INTERNATIONAL RELATIONS
IN INSTITUTIONS OF HIGHER EDUCATION
IN THE SOUTH

Studies in
Universities and World Affairs —

International Relations in Institutions of Higher Education in the South

FRED COLE — *1912*

Academic Vice-President, Tulane University

AMERICAN COUNCIL ON EDUCATION · *Washington, D. C.*

*Prepared for the Carnegie Endowment for International Peace,
the Southern Regional Education Board, and the Southern
University Conference; published by the
American Council on Education*

LIBRARY OF CONGRESS CATALOG CARD NO. 58–7687

PRINTED IN THE UNITED STATES OF AMERICA

FOREWORD

THIS STUDY differs from others in the series in that the approach is regional rather than topical. In the four volumes that have been published thus far, the role of colleges and universities in world affairs has been explored through discussions of selected topics: the contribution of extracurricular experiences to a broad outlook; the foreign student on the American campus; the relevant techniques of adult education; the training of specialists. Cutting across topical lines, this fifth volume is a preliminary survey of attitudes and practices in the teaching of international relations throughout the South. In the three remaining volumes of the series, now in preparation, the topical approach will be resumed.

In selecting an area that would provide a good cross section of the country for study, the South was a logical choice. Here three points of view converged: the broad perspective of the Southern Regional Education Board, accustomed over the years to considering the academic resources of the area as a whole; the keen interest of the Southern University Conference in the problem to be studied; and the traditional concern of the Carnegie Endowment for International Peace with research and instruction in the international field. Fortunately, all three points of view were represented by Dr. Fred Cole of Tulane University, who was invited to direct the survey. To this task Dr. Cole brought not only his experience as professor of history and dean of the College of Liberal Arts and Sciences at Tulane but also an editorial background extending through a score of years following his graduation from Louisiana State University. In the course of the study which this volume records, he was called away to serve with the Ford Foundation, returning to Tulane to resume his responsibilities as academic vice-president of the university.

As Dr. Cole points out, the survey was conceived as an initial inquiry into the prevailing and highly varied status of the teaching of international relations in one section of the United States. It was not designed as an exhaustive analysis, institution by institution, but rather as a springboard from which further inquiry might be launched as occasion arose. From the very fact that questions of current status were raised, a decade after the close of World War II, it may be assumed that teaching in the field has been strengthened throughout the area. Accordingly, the first objective of the study has already been attained. It is the hope of the sponsors that publication of the study will provide a second stimulus, leading to continued improvement in attitudes and practices. Perhaps additional ways may be found to implement the study still further and so maintain steady progress in this significant sector of higher education.

JOHN E. IVEY, JR.
For the Southern Regional Education Board

ANNE GARY PANNELL
For the Southern University Conference

JOSEPH E. JOHNSON, PRESIDENT
Carnegie Endowment for International Peace

EDITOR'S PREFACE

THE IMPORTANCE of educating young Americans in the complexities of international relations grows more apparent with each passing year. Problems and programs of such education about world affairs are receiving increasing attention on a widening scale. The series of volumes on "American Universities and World Affairs," of which this is one, deals intimately with questions which higher education in the modern world cannot avoid.

Beginning in 1950 the Carnegie Endowment for International Peace developed a program by which some seventy American colleges and universities undertook studies and appraisals of their resources and academic activities bearing on world affairs. This program was decentralized; each cooperating institution worked on such aspects of a self-study as seemed to it significant. However, in one region of the nation, a general analysis of the work in international relations was attempted. The Southern Regional Education Board's interest in comprehensive planning for the further development of higher education within the fourteen states of its jurisdiction, the concern of the Southern University Conference with teaching international affairs, and the program of self-studies sponsored by the Carnegie Endowment were joined in the sponsorship of the study which is reported in this volume.

Dr. Fred Cole, serving as chairman of a committee established by the Southern Regional Education Board and the Southern University Conference, became also the representative in the South of the Carnegie Endowment's program. In the project developed under his direction were brought together a series of studies on which colleges had individually embarked as well as the questionnaire and interview enterprises undertaken on a regional basis by Dr. Cole and his staff. The result is an over-all account of education for international relations in Southern institutions of higher education. This reporting volume thus embodies a unique approach in the general group of surveys sponsored by the Endowment as the basis of the series of volumes published by the American Council on Education. In this volume Dr. Cole gives a regional focus to the analysis of "universities and world affairs." His data have value not only for Southern institutions, but as a cross-sectional analysis worthy of consideration in all regions of the United States. Many of the conclusions he draws and the observations he makes are as applicable to the Midwest or the Pacific Coast area or to other areas of the country as they are to the South. It is the cross-sectional analysis of all types of institutions rather than the strictly geographic region of his concern that gives this volume its major value in the series of which it is a part.

The volumes in the series are listed on page ii of this volume. It includes a number of topical reports based in part on the institutional self-surveys sponsored by the Carnegie Endowment and in larger part upon related researches known to the authors of these volumes. The series is predicated upon the conviction that higher education in the United States has a critical role in the ultimate conduct of our foreign relations—that role is evidenced by curricular instruction on world affairs, by research, by contributions to adult education, by a college way of life which widens students' horizons, by exchanges of students and professors, and by the training of specialists in international relations. The volumes of this series deal with these various phases of a twentieth-century development and a responsibility which colleges and universities cannot escape.

To this series of reports, Dr. Cole's volume adds a new dimension. It reports issues and considerations which should give us concern, not only in the South but throughout the nation.

HOWARD E. WILSON

January 24, 1958

PREFACE

THE RESPONSIBILITY for leadership which has been thrust upon the United States imposes heavy demands upon American citizens. It calls upon them to exercise wisdom in matters concerning which they have previously had little knowledge and less experience. They cannot, like certain peoples on the opposite side of the world, leave all the decisions and policies up to their leaders. In a democracy the people not only demand to know where their leaders are taking them, but often they wish to—indeed, they must—point the direction and signal the turn.

Higher education is assuming a significant share of the burden of raising the level of knowledge about international relations. The necessity to do so is clearly recognized in most colleges and universities. Unfortunately, however, this recognition is comparatively recent. Like the government, the colleges for many years tended to emphasize American affairs almost to the exclusion of foreign affairs. The need to modify this tradition was becoming slowly apparent during the grim prelude of the 1930's. Then the impact of World War II and its aftermath brought pressures upon the colleges and universities for hurried steps to expand curricular, cocurricular, and extracurricular activities related to international affairs.

Americans were transformed quite precipitately from half-interested spectators to principal actors on the world stage. It was therefore difficult to devise a means of teaching them quickly the lines and techniques which other peoples had spent centuries in learning. Understandably, the educational programs and activities evolved under the urgencies of American reaction to international crises were not all equally effective. In a somewhat haphazard fashion, courses were added here and there to cover issues of the day. As one area of the world after another turned out to be the contemporary "hot spot," scholars who were specialists or who had the potential of becoming specialists were sought out to develop area study programs. Whereas Europe had once been the foreign area of primary interest to scholars, programs in Far Eastern, Asian, and Latin-American studies were invigorated and increased in number.

Different kinds of formal programs were tried experimentally: special departments of international relations, subject majors in traditional disciplines with emphasis upon international affairs or upon a special area, multidisciplinary majors, interdisciplinary seminars in world affairs or in the affairs of a particular area, and so on. Field trips, lecture series, faculty and student exchange programs, international relations clubs, and other types of activities were multiplied in attempts to extend knowledge and interest in world affairs to larger numbers of students. Many of these programs and developments are reported and analyzed in other volumes of this series, "Studies in Universities and World Affairs."

Some activities evolved under pressure of those critical years have been apparently fruitful. Others are subject to adverse criticism. All require evaluation in the light of subsequent experience, educational and international.

In keeping with the scholarly tradition of objectivity, questions are being constantly raised concerning the effectiveness of activities proposed and initiated to teach Americans more about international affairs. Are the would-be specialists being given proper training? Is good use being made of educational facilities to enhance the knowledge of world affairs among *all* students? Which programs have been most profitable? Which should be expanded, and which curtailed?

A starting point in determining what ought to be done is to determine what now is being done and to attempt weighing the effectiveness of present activities. Efforts to determine the status and effectiveness of current activities have been made by individuals and organizations in the recent past. Indebted to these, the present study was launched in the belief that there is need for further appraisal based upon comparable data and expressed purposes.

The study reported here was initiated in 1954 as a result of the collaboration of three organizations—the Southern Regional Education Board, the Southern University Conference, and the Carnegie Endowment for International Peace. Two specific factors animated the undertaking of the study and, in part, set it off from its predecessors. The first is the special interest of the Southern Regional Education Board and the Southern University Conference in matters pertaining to college curricula in the American South.[1] The second—and here lay the basis for cooperation with the Carnegie Endowment—was that previous studies have been focused primarily upon either a specific institution, or a small number of the larger or specializing institutions in the United States or abroad.

The study of a specific institution usually does not lend itself to analyses from which generalizations about the teaching of international relations may be made. Concentration upon a relatively small number of specializing institutions can reveal what is being done to train the potential expert in foreign policy, but it must leave unanswered many questions concerning education in international relations for the great majority of college and university students who will never be professionally involved in foreign affairs. Most of these will, however, in their responsibilities as citizens, be called upon to make judgments deeply affecting the conduct of our foreign relations; and others may in various manners become participants in foreign affairs operations or policymaking after their educational training has been completed. It was decided, therefore, to make a regional study of education in international relations which would embrace both the specializ-

[1] For the purposes of this survey, the Southern region includes Alabama, Arkansas, Florida, Georgia, Kentucky, Louisiana, Maryland, Mississippi, North Carolina, Oklahoma, South Carolina, Tennessee, Texas, and Virginia. These fourteen states are the signatories of the Southern Regional Education Compact.

ing institutions, actual or potential, and those whose resources or objectives lead them to treat international relations as a part of general education.

The purpose of the regional study described in the following pages was to obtain information about the resources available in Southern colleges and universities related to the teaching and study of international relations. To describe the resources available, it was necessary to consider what constituted a resource: a course—or an extracurricular activity or a special facility—might be considered by one person to be an essential resource and by another to be a waste of time. Determination of available resources led inevitably, therefore, to a consideration of educated opinion about what international relations, as a subject field in colleges and universities, is and ought to be.

The results of the study, then, emerge from both fact and opinion. To obtain the data questionnaires were sent to the accredited colleges and universities in every Southern state, and personal interviews were conducted with a variety of individuals and groups in many of the universities and colleges of the region. By raising the same or similar questions from institution to institution, comparable, though by no means conforming, data were obtained. Based on these data, generalizations were made; these are presented as objectively as possible. In addition to a summary, some suggestions are presented as to means for evaluating the present and future effectiveness of international relations programs in colleges and universities.

This survey results from the work of a number of individuals and groups. It is not feasible to list all the persons who participated directly or indirectly in the undertaking. Dr. Richard W. Sterling joined the staff shortly after the initiation of the survey and worked closely with the director for a little more than a year. As a specialist in international relations, he was able to give assistance of particular importance in the interview phase of the study and in bringing to bear upon the findings the point of view of a student and practitioner of international relations. Others who made significant direct contributions were M. M. Kreeger, Mrs. Villa Cox, Mrs. Lucie Lee Wing, Mrs. Grace Curtis, and Dr. Mary Lystad. Because there was lack of continuity in association by some of those who contributed to the survey, it is, I believe, appropriate to acknowledge with deep appreciation their contribution and at the same time to assume full responsibility for the faults in presentation and the interpretation where it is inadequate.

FRED COLE

January 1958

CONTENTS

LIST OF TABLES

1

General Considerations

THE TERM "international relations" has, unfortunately, different meanings to different persons. Varying interpretations were made by the academicians whose opinions were sought during this study. To maintain a consistent focus we have, for the general purposes of this survey, defined international relations in a college curriculum as constituting those studies which can lead to an understanding of contacts, connections, and intercourse between sovereign states in the modern world.

No claim is made that this is an ideal definition. It does, however, have two advantages for the task at hand. First, it proposes that the core of international relations is political—it pertains to the functions or exercise of governmental authority. This proposition, which is in accordance with the thinking of the majority of those to whom the matter has been of concern, establishes a criterion of relevancy and at least some limit to the extent of the inquiry. For example, unless a given course of study is aiding the student to gain an insight into the relationships among states, it cannot be regarded as contributing to his understanding of international relations.

Second, it recognizes that there are many paths to political understanding. Such an explicit recognition is imperative, not simply because it is true, but also for very practical reasons. The status of international relations, as a relative newcomer to the academic fold, has meant that no standard manner of teaching it has yet been developed. This fact expresses itself in both substantive and administrative terms. Substantively, there is great variation in the components of specialized programs in the relatively few colleges and universities which offer them. In the much larger number of institutions giving some work in international relations as part of the general curriculum, there is great variation in the nature of these offerings. Administratively, the kinds of departments that participate both in the specialized programs and in the teaching of general offerings also are marked in their variation. In this situation it was not possible to make any rigid assumptions concerning the types of courses or departments that ought to be discussed during interviews and discussions relative to the present study.

Scope and Procedures of the Survey

The South is a very large region. To undertake a survey of international relations education in the higher institutions of so large an area necessitated making a selection of those factors which were to be given emphasis. Consequently, primary attention was given to the academic aspects of the field and particularly to graduate and undergraduate teaching programs and course offerings, since obviously formal education in the field is one of the central concerns. Matters such as international exchange of faculty and students and general extracurricular activities are of peculiar importance to the study of international relations, but they are extensively treated in other volumes in this series.

The general orientation of the research program was toward determining the present status of academic activities in the field of international relations. Inevitably, there were two approaches.

1. Personal interviews and discussions were conducted during 1954–55, principally by a specialist in international relations, with the intention of obtaining from faculty members and others their assessments of academic activities in international relations and of international relations itself as a field for special study. One of the main purposes of the extensive interview program was to elicit discussion of substantive issues among teachers in the South and then to reflect the discussion in this report. During the course of personal visits to the campuses, more than three hundred inter-

views were held. The interviews, primarily with faculty members but also with some students, were not restricted to those actually giving or taking courses in international relations. Such a restriction would have been highly unrealistic, not only because many different fields are directly or indirectly contributory to international relations study, but also because the views of those less immediately concerned than international relations teachers were essential in order to gain a perspective of the role of international relations in the total university curriculum. Hence anthropologists, geographers, teachers of law and philosophy as well as political scientists, historians, and economists were among the interviewees.

Time limitations prevented visits to all the institutions which participated in the survey. Because those offering advanced degrees in political science afforded the most abundant and varied work relevant to international relations study, at both the graduate and undergraduate levels, most of the group whose political science programs were of some years' standing were visited. At the same time the survey's concern with the problem of the smaller college and international relations in general education required that the interview program be broad enough to include as many as possible of the institutions which were not centers of graduate instruction. Approximately 7 percent of these institutions, believed by the principal interviewer to constitute a reasonably representative sample, were visited. Altogether, visits were made to thirty-seven campuses in the Southern area.

2. In order to obtain comparable information of a factual nature about the academic facilities available in Southern institutions for the study of international relations, questionnaires were sent in 1954 to 273 accredited four-year institutions in the South. The accrediting agencies were the Southern, Middle States, and North Central Associations of Colleges and Secondary Schools.

The institutions were divided into four categories, according to size and complexity of organization. Four questionnaires were prepared, with a common core, varied to cover the offerings in each of the four types of institutions. Table 1 summarizes the definitions of the groups and the questionnaires sent to institutions of each group. Questionnaire I, the basis for all the other questionnaires, is presented in Appendix A.

TABLE 1

HIGHER INSTITUTIONS IN THE SOUTH GROUPED BY TYPE OF OFFERING IN POLITICAL SCIENCE AND SURVEY QUESTIONNAIRE SENT

Group	Definition*	Questionnaire Sent
I	Institutions with graduate programs leading at least to a master's degree in political science	I and II
II	Institutions with undergraduate majors in political science	II
III	Institutions with no undergraduate major in political science	III
IV	Technical or professional schools with no undergraduate major in political science	IV

*In each case categorization of an institution was based on information published in its 1953 catalogue.

Group I consisted of institutions with graduate schools offering, according to their catalogues, at least a master's degree in political science. To obtain complete information from this group, both Questionnaires I and II were sent. They were identical in content, except that questions were directed toward the graduate level in Questionnaire I and the undergraduate level in Questionnaire II. They consisted of questions concerning departments in which courses related to international relations were given; special programs and how administered; degrees or certificates granted; detailed lists of courses showing title, frequency of offering, length, whether required or elective; texts used, and additional information available in bibliographies, syllabi, etc.; additional aids to teaching; field trips; awards (fellowships, assistantships, and the like); specific questions about existing formal programs in international relations, their origin and future; faculty background; and information on research.

Group II included institutions which had no graduate programs in political science but which, according to their catalogues, offered at least a major in political science. To this classification Questionnaire II was sent.

The institutions included in Group III were colleges offering, according to their catalogues, no undergraduate major in political science. Questionnaire III, designed for this classification, consisted of questions concerning the departments which offered courses related to international relations; lists of courses offered, showing length, frequency of offering, whether required or elective; supplementary instructional facilities available; future plans; and faculty background.

The smallest category of institutions questioned, Group IV, comprised the technical schools. Questionnaire IV, essentially the same as Questionnaire III, was sent to this group.

The questionnaire method admittedly has its drawbacks. No set of questions can be applied equally in a number of complex situations. The objective, however, was to gather comparable information. This method was, therefore, considered preferable to asking the institutions simply what they were doing in the field of international relations. The replies to specific questions make it possible to summarize data about facilities common to groups of institutions and to present a picture representing, to some degree, at least, various patterns of activities in Southern colleges and universities.

The results are reported principally in tabular form, with some amplification in the text. The statistical data reveal general activities in the field of international relations both in those institutions with special programs in the field and in those with few or no specialized offerings.

General Comments on the Questionnaire Respondents

Usable replies were received from 191 institutions.[1] This response—70 percent—was excellent for questionnaires of the length and complexity of those used in this survey. It demonstrates the cooperative spirit and interest of the Southern colleges and universities generally in the project. Also, as shown in Table 2, the proportion of replies was consistently distributed both geographically and according to categories of institutions. Because of the size and distribution of the return, it is believed that the totals based on the questionnaire materials may be given with some confidence that they are representative.

Generally speaking, questionnaires were sent directly to the chief administrative officer of each institution, who was asked to designate an appropriate person to fill out the questionnaire. Where there were organized programs or committees established for the consideration of problems in international relations study, the questionnaire materials usually were turned over to the chairman of the committee or the head of the program. Where there were no such formal facilities, the chairman or a member of the political science department, or, in the absence of a separate department, someone in the history department was designated to answer the questionnaire. It was not unusual, especially in the smaller institutions, for the questionnaire to be filled out by the liberal arts college dean or by the assistant dean. In a few cases, the materials were turned over to the registrar's office for completion. In some instances it was clear from the responses that several faculty members, either as a formal committee or as an informal temporary group, were called upon to assist in filling out the questionnaire. Because of the length and complexity of the questionnaires, there is little doubt that on most campuses cooperation was required of faculty members in addition to the one

[1] See Appendix B for a list of 193 institutions, by states, from which questionnaires were received. The questionnaires from two of the institutions were received too late to include their data in the group tabulations.

TABLE 2

DISTRIBUTION OF AND RESPONSE TO SURVEY QUESTIONNAIRE, BY STATES

STATE	GROUP I No. Sent	GROUP I No. Retd.	GROUP II No. Sent	GROUP II No. Retd.	GROUP III No. Sent	GROUP III No. Retd.	GROUP IV No. Sent	GROUP IV No. Retd.	TOTAL No. Sent	TOTAL No. Retd.	TOTAL Percent Retd.
Alabama	1	1	7	7	7	2	2	2	17	12	71
Arkansas	1	1	7	4	1	0	2	2	11	7	64
Florida	4	3*	0	0	6	4	1	1	11	8	73
Georgia	3	3	4	3	16	12	1	1	24	19	79
Kentucky	2	2	9	6	5	4	0	0	16	12	75
Louisiana	2	2	7	6	5	4	0	0	14	12	86
Maryland	2	1	6	4	9	7	1	0	17	12	71
Mississippi	1	1	5	5	6	4	2	2	13	10	77
North Carolina	2	2	7	4	19	12	2	2	30	20	67
Oklahoma	2	1	4	2	8	5	0	0	14	8	57
South Carolina	1	1	7	6	11	4	0	0	19	11	58
Tennessee	3	3	11	7	9	7	1	1	24	18	75
Texas	13	9	15	7	10	7	1	1	39	24	62
Virginia	2	2	12	10	7	4*	3	2	24	18	75
Total	39	32	101	71	119	76	14	12	273	191	70
Percent Retd.	82		70		64		86		70		

*The questionnaire of one institution in the state was received too late to include data in the group tabulations.

7

designated as chiefly responsible in order to answer some of the questions.

Design of the Presentation of the Questionnaire Results

Table 3 presents statistically the proportion of each type of institution represented in the total number participating in this phase of the survey. It may be well for the reader, at this point, to turn briefly to Appendix B (pages 158–63), where the names of the institutions in each group are listed. A quick glance at the lists by those reasonably familiar with Southern colleges and universities will go far in bringing to life the accurate but colorless definitions of groups given in Table 1. Thus, "Group I" may suggest the University of Texas or Virginia, or Duke or Vanderbilt as typical examples, rather than simply a group of unnamed schools where both undergraduate and graduate programs leading to a degree in political science are offered. Similarly, the names in Appendix B may assist the reader in typifying the members of Groups II, III, and IV.

TABLE 3

NUMBER AND PERCENTAGE OF INSTITUTIONS
REPLYING TO QUESTIONNAIRE, CLASSIFIED BY GROUP

GROUP No.	INSTITUTIONS	
	No.	*Percent*
I	32*	17
II	71	37
III	76	40
IV	12	6
Total	191	100

*The list of Group I institutions on pp. 158–59 indicates which of the 32 institution returned only the undergraduate or only the graduate questionnaire.

Group I institutions, comprising most of the large Southern universities, generally reported more facilities, more personnel, more courses, more programs, and more research related to international relations than did the institutions in the other groups. However, comparisons only of the *amount* of activity concerned with international relations would yield little information not already either known or presumed. The survey staff therefore decided to use the following question as one of the criteria in developing the statistical analyses: How do the four types of institutions differ in their utilization of the facilities they have or might have available, leaving aside total quantity? If, for example, the larger universities report that they offer twice as many courses in or related to international relations as the smaller colleges, the following questions might be asked: In each group, what proportion of the courses offered are in political science? In history? In economics? What is the comparative emphasis given to European studies? To Latin-American and other area studies?

Throughout the tabular materials that follow, then, are analyses not only of the *number* of departments, courses, faculty members, and so on, but also of the differing characteristics, from group to group, of the facilities and personnel available for the study of international relations. The survey staff hoped that through this means the quantitative data presented would yield some insight into the qualitative differences among the groups of institutions in their activities related to international relations.

This report aspires to be a systematic effort to assay in broad fashion present academic activities in international relations in Southern higher institutions, as well as a variety of opinions concerning the merit or lack of merit of these activities. It does not pretend to be an exhaustive study of international relations education in the South nor can it hope to present definitive solutions to the complex problems with which it must deal. An initial survey in an amorphous field such as international relations cannot answer all the questions when many of the questions themselves are still to be determined.

As originally planned, one section of the survey (interviews) was envisioned as subjective and the other section (questionnaires) as objective. It was intended to present these sections separately, making a volume of two distinct parts. The subjective element, however, proved to have a noticeable effect upon the questionnaire data. The individuals who did the actual work of preparing the answers to the questionnaire varied widely in their academic backgrounds. Some were specialists in international relations; some had comparatively tenuous connections with the field. Some construed the questions more broadly than others. There were differences in the patterns of answers from different types of institutions, which suggested that different criteria of interpretation had been employed. It was decided therefore to combine the presentation of the two sections, even though the interviews and questionnaires had not been set up in parallel form.

The survey staff and the advisory committee hope that the material presented will be considered not as a guide but as a beginning to continuous study of a highly important field. And, if this report succeeds in stimulating both the expert and the interested layman to a continuing examination of the role of international relations in the educational process, it will have achieved its major purpose.

Summary

In this survey, international relations is held to mean all studies which may lead to an understanding of contacts, connections, and intercourse between modern sovereign states. The core of such studies is political, but there is wide variation in departments and courses involved.

The survey was concentrated especially upon teaching programs and course offerings, graduate and undergraduate. Information was gathered by means of personal interviews with faculty members and with some students and through questionnaires. The institutions were divided into four groups according to type and offerings in political science, and the questionnaires were adapted to the characteristics of the respective groups. Questionnaires were sent to 273 accredited four-year colleges, and the replies of 191 institutions are used in the tabular analyses in the chapters which follow.

2

Background of Intangibles

ONE OF THE primary problems of international relations as a field of study is its catholicity. It is, indeed, a broad and varied field. However, it is not unique among the social sciences in having to ask, "Where is the beginning and the end?" It faces problems analogous to those of economics, for example, which cannot avoid the question as to where economics shades into sociology or psychology. The difference comes at another question level. Presumably, economics can legitimately encompass the economic aspects of anything. Can international relations consider effectively the international aspects of anything it chooses?

A few of those participating in the survey apparently would answer this question in the affirmative. Thus, one college, in responding to the questionnaire, stated that physical education was designed to give the student some understanding of international relations because sports involve international competition. Another college listed home economics as relevant because classwork included study of the World Health Organization. Still another mentioned considerable work in home economics because home economists were in demand as technicians for positions abroad and some instruction was given in home economics as practiced in foreign countries.

This latter consideration introduces a further problem, reflected at another level by the interchangeability of such terms as international relations, foreign affairs, and world affairs. "International" is often equated with "foreign," and the conclusion is frequently drawn that any subject which concerns itself with phenomena outside the limits of the United States is *ipso facto*

11

relevant to international relations. Logically, all such phenomena can be grouped under the heading of "foreign affairs." This interpretation of international relations would place within its purview every conceivable human activity geographically removed from American shores.

This construction, however, destroys any semblance of a coherent approach to the field. The annexation of every academic discipline as it applies to areas outside the United States would imply that the student must address himself to a diversity of intellectual problems which no one individual could hope to consider, let alone master. Finally, it imposes an obviously artificial geographical line that would cut across what are at least theoretically universal disciplines.

From another point of view the inclusion of such courses as music, literature, art, even of household arts and sports forms in other countries and at different periods of time, can be of value to the student of international relations in the sense that he gains thereby an increased understanding of the diverse cultures and traditions with which he must deal. But the great majority would agree that the student of international relations wishes to gain this understanding as a means to an end, and that the end is insight into the interactions of diverse cultures. The great problem of our time concerns the situations that arise from these interactions. The central questions are how and why they produce conflicts and adjustments and what might be done to ameliorate the conflicts.

It must be remembered, however, that we are considering primarily international and not intercultural relations. A country such as the United States or the Soviet Union may display greater cultural diversities than two sovereign countries of the Middle East or Latin America. A resident of Manhattan learning American square dancing is studying a subject which is more alien to his environment, certainly, than is the modern British drama. And if we go back in time, a foreign culture may not really be any more foreign to us than to many other people. Americans are the heirs of the higher elements of Sumerian, Egyptian, Hebrew, Hellenic, and Roman culture as truly as are any present inhabitants of the Mediterranean Basin.

Granting, then, that such tangential courses may impart desirable background, it nonetheless remains true that they constitute background only. Unless they are combined with studies which focus more directly on the central problems of international relations, they cannot—most would agree—be said to contribute to the student's direct understanding of the field.

The majority of those questioned during interviews agreed that the crucial conflicts and adjustments generated by interaction express themselves primarily *politically*. Since states are the chief actors at the international level, conflicts and adjustments concerning the exercise of governmental authority must be the center of attention. Thus, courses that include study of international interaction can be labeled as training in international relations only if they themselves constitute or are combined with studies which center on major interstate political problems. At this point, then, it is necessary to narrow the definition at least to the extent that we may proceed on the basis that international relations is not the study of the international aspects of just anything. It is a field in which effort culminates in an analysis of political interaction at the international level.

Many scholars believe an educational institution should use this criterion to measure its efforts in the field of international relations. A relative abundance of course offerings may provide necessary or desirable background, but does not by itself constitute adequate training in international relations. This applies not only to the courses on the periphery cited above but also to those, such as history or economics of foreign countries, which are much closer to the center of focus. We shall return later to a consideration of the relationship of this kind of course offering to the core of international relations studies.

Effect of Values on the Field

Another major problem in the study of international relations is the role of normative ideas. The problem finds expression in many ways. One is the frequent practice of making the terms "understanding international relations" and "international understanding" interchangeable. Those who follow this practice usually conceive the mission of teaching international relations to be one of freeing the student from parochialism and leading him toward the goal of world-mindedness. Such an objective can be a purely utilitarian one of encouraging the student to broaden his horizons. But more often than not it is coupled with ethically normative goals. A similar problem exists in the teaching of political science. Those who cite citizenship training as a main objective are opposed by those most eager to justify the designation of the field as a science, lest the subject become overly susceptible to the practices of indoctrination.

An example of the ambiguities that can arise from the use of such terms as international understanding is provided in a report by the American Council on Education devoted to education for international understanding. The report stated that institutions of higher learning were responsible for developing a determination to build for peace and for fostering world-mindedness. The report observed, on the other hand, that "international understanding" may "also be defined from the viewpoint of the social anthropologist as an ability to anticipate the behavior of people individually or in groups, in the situations in which they are placed."[1]

The latter interpretation of international understanding is apparently preferred by the great majority of teachers of international relations in the South. These teachers believe that greater knowledge of international relations would not necessarily imply an increased friendliness toward other peoples. It could hardly be the province of the international relations teacher to incite enmity. Yet it would be his duty to identify both causes and areas of international conflict and to confront the student with a de-

[1] Howard L. Nostrand and Francis J. Brown (eds.), *The Role of Colleges and Universities in International Understanding* (Washington: American Council on Education, 1949), p. 31.

tailed and hence, presumably, a more impelling knowledge that his country has actual and potential enemies as well as friends abroad. To argue otherwise would suggest that a better understanding of Communist and Fascist regimes could or ought to lead to a feeling of greater friendliness toward them.

As one teacher put it, "International understanding does not mean likes or dislikes but understanding of other peoples and the problems they face." While he speaks for the majority who wish to avoid normative implications of "international understanding," there is nonetheless a normative problem in this statement as well. The problem is illustrated by another teacher's assertion that it was necessary to "create an attitude of genuine tolerance and intelligent consideration of world affairs." There is agreement, then, that if it is not the mission of the international relations teacher to inculcate friendly feelings toward the rest of the world, he certainly should combat misunderstanding caused by either prejudice or ignorance. Here the idea of "ought" is primarily utilitarian in the sense that hate and passion are poor guides to policy. But ethical considerations cannot be entirely divorced from that aspect of teaching which seeks to replace indifference, suspicion, or active dislikes with tolerance and understanding. There seems to be ethical good as well as utilitarian value in combating parochialism.

All these considerations are related to the familiar arguments about realism and idealism in international relations. This debate has gone on in various forms since the beginning of organized human activity, but for our purpose it is important to note that it has played a significant role in international relations as an academic subject in the United States since the First World War. George Kennan has suggested that international relations teaching has shared a general American distrust of the idea of power, and has tended to ignore the power concept in instructing the young. This view was echoed by a Southern teacher who claimed that moralistic goals are often presupposed in courses in international relations. These goals would lead students from "selfish isolationism" to an internationalism compounded of good will toward other peoples, a belittling and deprecation of national sovereignty, and a belief that force in international conflicts could be quickly and easily eliminated, particularly if all nations would agree to subordinate themselves to a supranational authority.

The effects of utopianism in international relations are illustrated not only in teaching but also in terms of public attitudes toward concrete issues of foreign policy. There are indications that the more educated groups have been more "internationalist" and optimistic in their views about peace prospects than the less educated have been. From evidence he gathered, Gabriel Almond generalized that

one may classify young people, women, the upper income groups, the college-educated and the urban population as more inclined to foreign policy idealism, optimism, and internationalism. The older generations, the males, the lower income groups, those with grade school education, and the rural population tend to be more inclined to cynicism, pessimism, isolationism, and nationalism.[2]

If these generalizations are acceptable, then Robert A. Dahl's suggestion[3] that internationalism is sometimes simply an attitude which may be unrelated to reality can be accepted as an admonition. It is, however, questionable whether this kind of "internationalism" or philosophy of "international understanding" is as prevalent in the international relations classroom as Mr. Kennan and others imply. In an appraisal of the interwar period of international relations studies, William T. R. Fox emphasized that the subject had come a long way from the time when it concentrated on "good" things such as techniques of pacific settlement, and underplayed "bad" things such as power politics.[4]

As far as the South is concerned, there is much evidence to indi-

[2] Almond, *The American People and Foreign Policy* (New York: Harcourt, Brace & Co., 1950), p. 129.

[3] Dahl, *Congress and Foreign Policy* (New York: Harcourt, Brace & Co., 1950), p. 76.

[4] Fox, "Interwar International Research: The American Experience," *World Politics,* October 1949, pp. 67, 74.

cate that idealism in international relations study has faded into the background. One Southern teacher, agreeing that the earlier teaching of international relations had been too "Pollyanna-ish," said his recent publications on international organization were intended to be somber and that students must learn to approach the problems of this field with realism. Another teacher said he had all but abandoned the teaching of international law because he believed legal concepts had only the remotest relationship to the actual conduct of nations' foreign policies. Only a single teacher among all those interviewed expressed the belief that students ought to be taught to see the need for "international government." Another, also an isolated voice, complained that there is too much stress on diplomacy and not enough on international cooperation and peace efforts.

If the kinds of textbooks used in international relations courses are any guide, the decline of idealism is little open to dispute. One of the books reported most frequently as required was Hans Morgenthau's *Politics Among Nations,* regarded by many as the archadvocate of "power politics." Indeed, many would argue that most international relations texts currently on the market are "realist." Certainly, it would be surprising to find in any of them the ethical overtones accompanying the denunciations of balance of power and secret diplomacy which characterized some of the earlier texts. It seems safe to say, then, that the international relations student who digests the content of most of today's textbooks will not be idealistic in the sense of glossing over the factors of power and national self-interest.

The virtual disappearance of the "one-world" spirit in international relations teaching is reflected also in student attitudes and interests. One teacher observed that "international relations classes once were battlefields. Now they are cemeteries—probably because the problems now seem too huge and defiant of solution. The typical student attitude nowadays is: 'Why study government or foreign policy? We can have no control over it.'" This statement in various forms was made again and again in the interviews. The majority of teachers characterized the attitude of the great bulk of students toward the study of international relations as one of profound apathy. Student apathy was said not to be restricted to international relations; it extended to political science and other fields touching upon areas which might call for a personal commitment on the part of a student. A Southern dean spoke for many when he said, "This is a cautious generation."

Many contrasted the present situation with the early postwar years during which the presence of veterans, stimulated by their wartime experiences, made for active interest in international relations. Others contrasted it with the 1930's. Some pointed out that before Pearl Harbor international relations classes were one of the many forums for the great debate on whether the United States would or would not have to participate in the great affairs of the world. Today, these observations run, this debate is dead, and no great issue has risen to take its place; it has been supplanted instead by a passive internationalism in the sense of an unemotional acceptance of the necessity for American involvement in all aspects of international relations.

There are some exceptions to this general picture. Many of those interviewed claimed that student interest in international relations is greater than it was fifteen years ago, although there was no dissent that the era of the GI at college was the high point of interest in the postwar years. More than one teacher, however, looked back with nostalgia to the days when there were "a few pacifists and Marxists" to liven up the classroom. Today's student was described as only infrequently holding strong convictions making for vigorous and creative discussions.

Current investigations of international relations doubtless have benefited from the fact that the classroom is generally no longer a forum for the clash of hotly controversial opinions. But the replacement of passion by indifference hardly can be regarded as an unmixed blessing. This is particularly true for a subject in which normative problems must and do play a tremendous role. The international relations teacher is dealing with such emotion- and norm-laden symbols as patriotism, violence, deception, and arbitrary action. He cannot deny the heritage of his field as an academic subject with its genesis in the fervent desire to stop men from destroying themselves in war. Nor can he be blind to the fact that he must analyze and interpret issues that are continually described and debated the world over in terms of good and evil.

One teacher said that the student must learn to consider the problem of order in international society without clinging to utopian ideas. Another asserted that the greatest problem of international relations is the interrelationship of power and human values; ethics and power must be considered together. Still another teacher affirmed that norm and reality constitute a central problem in international relations: one must never be considered to the exclusion of the other. These voices indicate that the problem of moral judgment in international relations is not everywhere being shunted aside in favor of a strictly "power" analysis.

It is likely that most international relations teachers in the South agree that a healthy balance of critical realism and idealism is necessary in the teaching of this subject. If such agreement can be assumed, it may presage a more profound appraisal of the role of morality in the relations of states than the utopian internationalism which characterized so much of the earlier teaching of international relations. Such an appraisal might do much to infuse new life into the international relations classroom. Certainly it can play a significant role in challenging the student to examine and refine his value preferences.

Some consideration may be given here to the public pressures that affect the teaching of international relations. The issue of norm and reality is obviously not confined to the campus; and international relations is a subject that must deal with, and is affected by, such controversial phenomena as the use of force, world communism, the isolationism-internationalism complex, xenophobia and chauvinism, nationalism, and supranational organization.

Given the state of public anxiety and embittered partisanship at the time of the interviews, it is little wonder that teachers in this field felt themselves to be particularly exposed to public pressures. In this atmosphere it is surprising that there were so few concrete instances of such pressures uncovered by the survey. At only five of the thirty-seven campuses visited did someone fail to mention the subject of public pressure, but in most cases the pressure was either covert or failed to affect directly the teaching of international relations. Many asserted that they felt subject to no pressures at all. Of those who did feel such pressures, the following were typical statements: "The [local] press is very hostile to 'world-mindedness,' but there have been no attacks specifically against the University of ———— and its teaching of international relations." "There is certainly an atmosphere of uneasiness. Students often preface statements with such phrases as: 'Now, I don't want to sound subversive, but. . . .'" "Students shy away from preparation for government work and the Foreign Service because they are in disrepute." "It is more difficult to teach international relations now. I feel a subconscious inner censorship. It is difficult to be critical of certain phases of American foreign policy and I must fight a tendency to skip over these phases." "Some students are afraid to speak out or take controversial courses, but the problem has not reached major proportions on this campus." "There is no overt public pressure, but the pressure is there nevertheless. It is more difficult today to give an objective presentation of political science and international relations."

Only in a few instances were more extreme situations reflected. These included the voluntary abandonment of a controversial textbook at several places. In one state the legislature forbade the use of this book in state-supported institutions. At one place, it was reported that students in a course on the Soviet Union were reluctant to buy an assigned book by Lenin "because the salesman looked at them as though they were Reds." At another it was feared that an annual three-day institute for the discussion of international relations would have to be dropped because of public reactions to false charges that the previous years' speakers had been Communists. At this same college there had been administrative opposition to a proposed summer trip for students to visit the State Department in Washington and the U.N. in New York because of fear of public reaction. Another teacher stated that, "A lecture on Unesco will evoke half a dozen protests. . . . No matter what your record and other attitudes are, if you're for Unesco you're a Commie. —————— is a well-known conservative on campus, but that doesn't save him from being labeled a Red downtown." At still another campus a faculty member giving a public lecture on Unesco was interrupted by "an old girl—a college graduate at that—who began to shout and holler and brandish her umbrella in denunciation of the U.N."

It should be emphasized again that such extreme situations are by no means typical. But taken together with the more widespread instances of milder forms of pressures, they illustrate the thesis that international politics can create reactions which may interfere with one's capacity to evaluate events objectively.

Thus, the issue of subversion has been superimposed on the old conflict of isolationism and internationalism so that, in certain areas, anyone espousing a greater measure of international cooperation may be subject to accusations that he is following the Communist line. The absurdity of this free association of ideas does not detract from its seriousness. The problems which it creates probably cannot be completely mastered until the universities are able to deal successfully with the public confusion regarding their over-all role and significance. But in the meantime it should be noted that the teaching of international relations is likely to be one of the first to suffer in an atmosphere of suspicion and distrust. This view also was expressed in a number of reports by institutions in all parts of the country participating in the Carnegie Endowment's program of self-surveys of international relations on college and university campuses.

The "Communist" issue overshadows all the other sources of controversy which affect the field of international relations. But its association with the isolationist-internationalist quarrel testifies to the continuing, if reduced, vitality of the latter. Most of those who expressed themselves on the latter problem felt that the isolationist position had far less attraction for students than for the older generations. Only at a few campuses did those interviewed say that isolationist attitudes were present, and even in these places the consensus was that such attitudes were displayed by only a small number of students. Note has already been made, however, that the relative absence of isolationism does not imply the presence of a vigorous concern for international relations. Isolationism is, after all, a fairly complex idea, and the waning of an idea need not mean that its components have disappeared. Provincialism and xenophobia, elements present in most isolationist complexes, were mentioned much more frequently than isolationism itself. Indeed, at the majority of places where interviews were conducted, these two characteristics were stressed as major obstacles to more effective work in international relations. According to the interviews, the statement that anything foreign is suspect may be regarded as the typical attitude of a large number of students on many Southern campuses.

One teacher's observation that "isolationism is an expression of resentment against the idea that certain problems are insoluble" was echoed by opinions from other campuses. Teachers commented that international relations are so complex that people tend to turn away from their consideration. One suggested, however, that "we are now in an incubating period. When we begin to grasp what the mechanisms for control are, then we may begin to generate some enthusiasm again." These statements would support the generalization that the old issue of whether or not to participate in the world's affairs is far simpler than the host of issues which arise when involvement is accepted and ways are sought to maximize the effectiveness of the participation.

The decline of idealism among teachers of international relations already has been noted. It is not surprising, then, to find that student idealism has also waned. Only very few of the teachers interviewed mentioned "idealistic illusions" as one of the important factors to be considered in international relations instruction. Even fewer mentioned pacifism as an issue in the classroom. While there is no reason to suppose that today's students have an affinity for warlike solutions to international problems, it seems certain that the widespread pacifism of the student generations of the 1930's has no parallel in the 1950's.

An important aspect of the idealist-pacifist syndrome of the 1930's was the tendency to condemn morally the power objectives of American foreign policy as revealed in American diplomatic history. This was part of the general repugnance for the phenomenon of self-interest. Not a single person interviewed mentioned this attitude as being in evidence today, although it may be assumed that it is present to some degree among the small minority which still embraces the pacifist and idealist approaches. Several teachers asserted that much of the articulate student criticism of American foreign policy today, while eschewing the "flag-waving" extreme, concerns the "bungling" of recent American diplomacy for its alleged failure to take a "tougher" line. As one teacher put it, "My students never seem to have heard of the idea that American foreign policy might have been subject to criticism *before* Yalta." Another teacher said that his students find it difficult to believe that American foreign policy has not always been ethically above reproach. Still another observed an "unconscious nationalism" among his students. They denied that United States foreign policy was influenced by selfish considerations, but they automatically argued policy issues from premises derived from such considerations. As a classic illustration of unconscious nationalism, one teacher said his students "all subscribed to the principle of the internationalization of major world waterways but were unwilling to let the principle apply to the Panama Canal." His point was "not that they should want to give up the Canal, but that they should not see the inconsistency of their position."

If one were to generalize on the basis of the interview discussions of student attitudes, "passive internationalism" combined with "unconscious nationalism" would probably be the outstanding characteristic which the average Southern student brings to the study of international relations. Articulate points of view ranging from pacifism to chauvinism and from isolationism to internationalism are exceptions. These exceptions apart, there seems to be little debate on the level of principle where there is passive deference to the idea of international cooperation. This near-unanimity breaks down at the level of concrete issues where the principle might seem to prejudice American interests; here the near-unanimity of unconscious nationalism holds sway. Probably most teachers of international relations would agree that one of their chief tasks is to aid the student in giving articulate form to his preferences and so to enable him to refine or reformulate them, as the case may be, in the light of a clearer idea of their consequences. To accomplish this, the teacher inevitably must deal with prejudices and sensibilities. If he fears to do so because of public pressures, real or imaginary, if he submits to an inner censor, it is clear that his teaching of international relations will suffer.

The Locale

The South has from time to time been identified as the most internationalist region of the United States. The traditional interest of the South in international trade and low tariffs is, of course, one of the main supports of this proposition. The results of various researchers indicate that this interest persists, although recently the tariff issue has become more debatable in the region.

But many people have contended that the sentiment for lower tariffs cannot be used as an indicator of an internationalist outlook, because it is an orientation with only a tangential relation to the great issues of world politics. Several studies have shown that the South is not internationalist in the sense of a conviction of the need to sacrifice some part of national sovereignty in order to achieve an international security system. On the contrary, they seem to show a "keep your powder dry" attitude. And it may be just this attitude which has helped to give the South the reputation for internationalism in the past. In this sense, internationalism apparently takes on the meaning of a belief that struggle is the way of the world and that in some struggles, at least, the United States has a vital stake which must be defended by force if need be. This attitude is perhaps best characterized as nationalism, and in the critical years before the United States' entry into World War II it evidently was this nationalism which helped to make the South consistently less isolationist than most other parts of the country. The issue then was not between altruistic idealists and hard-headed realists but turned on the question of intervention and nonintervention, or rather participation and nonparticipation. There were idealists and realists in both camps, and it is likely that the lack of a pacifist tradition in the South and the preparedness viewpoint turned the Southern realists to the side of participation.

Perhaps Southerners have arrived at an understanding of the United States' position similar to the explanation which Thucydides gave for the policy of Athens: "We assert that we are rulers in Hellas in order not to be subjects; liberators in Sicily that we may not be harmed by the Sicilians; that we are compelled to interfere in many things, because we have many things to guard against."

Some have asserted that running deeper than all of these relatively contemporary attitudes has been the South's own history which made it the only part of the United States to feel the full impact of war, having experienced defeat as well as victory. Because the South has experienced the results of unpreparedness, or, if you will, being under the victor's heel, it has, some believe, a greater tendency than other parts of the United States to wish the country prepared for emergencies both within its own borders and through alliances with friendly nations. In line with this view as well as with the South's primarily Anglo-Saxon ancestry among its leaders has been the frequent identification of

Southerners with British patterns and the sympathy of Southerners with Great Britain when it has been threatened. The South also has a higher percentage of native-born than most other regions. Where non-English-speaking communities are found, they are likely to represent indigenous populations or migrations of long ago, such as the French in Louisiana and the Germans in Texas. Conscious loyalties to ancestral homelands have faded with the passage of time. More recent immigrants have not formed residential colonies in Southern cities as they have in those of other sections. Moreover, group tensions in the South are centered overwhelmingly in relations between Negroes and whites or, in Texas, between "Americans" and the Spanish-speaking Indians or "mixed breeds" called Mexicans. Despite its nativism, the South probably sees comparatively little active discrimination because of national origin per se. Thus, there have been fewer significant groups in the South to identify themselves overtly with foreign countries or with ideologies associated with those countries. Whether or not one accepts these theses, there is much evidence to indicate that the South has not gone to the extremes of isolationism or utopian internationalism that have colored much of American foreign policy since 1914.

Over and above these observations, some of which are based on assessments of rather intangible attitudes and their sources, one clear fact concerning the South's role in international relations stands out. Because of the political situation in the South and the repeated re-election of Southern senators and representatives to Congress, Southern members of Congress frequently have gained the prerogatives of seniority. This has placed them in positions of political prestige and lawmaking power on congressional committees concerned with foreign relations. If there were no other facet of the South which differentiated it from other regions, the leadership of Southern congressmen on foreign relations committees would alone justify a special interest in the activities of Southern colleges and universities in international relations.

Summary

As many subjects may deal with material that overlaps national and cultural boundaries, it is necessary to narrow the definition of international relations. It is a field in which effort culminates in an analysis of political interaction at the international level.

The study or understanding of international relations is sometimes misconstrued by the lay public as implying "one-worldism" or sympathy with foreign ideologies. It is affected also by students' attitudes toward other peoples, by nationalistic feelings, and by pessimism as to the possibility of improving world conditions. The consensus of teachers in the field appears to be that although it is not their mission to inculcate friendly feelings toward the rest of the world, they should combat misunderstanding caused by prejudice or ignorance. To accomplish his purpose the teacher must deal with prejudices and sensibilities without self-censorship induced by fear of public pressures.

The Southern attitude toward international affairs has generally been acknowledgment that the United States must have active and extensive dealings with foreign countries, but at no sacrifice of American interests or sovereignty. The South has exhibited little of the extremes of either isolationism or idealistic internationalism which have been observable in other sections. Historical and ethnic factors may be largely responsible for the Southern outlook.

3

The Academic Status of International Relations

THE ISSUES AND illustrations presented in the last chapter demonstrate that value judgments are inextricably involved in the teaching of international relations. These value judgments together with the far-flung and amorphous boundaries of the subject —even granting that the core of study is political—lay the subject of international relations open to the charge that it is not a discipline and, in general, has a doubtful academic status.

A Discipline or What?

In order to discuss this criticism, a series of problems must be considered: Is there a standard content? Is there a distinct methodology? What is the relationship of international relations to the accepted disciplines? What are the problems of an interdisciplinary approach? Before such a consideration, it may be well to point out that international relations is not the only subject plagued by questions of its proper academic function and place.

SIMILAR PROBLEMS IN OTHER FIELDS

It has been claimed that international relations has no central core, that its students cannot master any one field of knowledge, and that the subjects to which it turns its attention are too diverse to permit an integrated treatment. But very similar criticisms have been leveled against older and more established fields. For example, Howard R. Bowen has written that the three major criticisms of economics have been that graduate programs attempt to crowd in too much because of proliferation of the subject matter; that students are so immersed in technicalities that they lack perspective and sense for politics or history; and that there is premature and excessive specialization.[1] These criticisms, Bowen asserted, lead to such questions as, "Should there be a common core and what should be its nature? What should be the role of economic theory, statistics, economic history?" Implying that no such core now exists, Bowen reported that more than 70 percent of graduate economics professors favored the establishment of a framework or point of departure.[2]

Another criticism of international relations is that it has developed no coherent methodology. It should be noted that the methodological problem in the social sciences as a whole has not been resolved to the satisfaction of many, at least insofar as the role of methodology in teaching programs is concerned. Elbridge Sibley, in his study of social science training, observed that:

Academic practice has lagged behind the development of social science. In undergraduate colleges comparatively little attention is paid to the processes by which knowledge in this field is created. . . . The same is in large measure true of the graduate schools. . . . These indictments must be qualified, for many social science departments are devoting increasing attention to training their students in research techniques; but it is still true that such training is generally the weakest aspect of the curriculum.[3]

These views, expressed in 1948, are repeated in particular reference to political science in the South more recently:

Nowhere is methodology recognized as a proper part of the undergraduate curriculum as it might be, and southern departments of political science give relatively little formal attention to either methodology or bibliography at the graduate level.[4]

[1] Bowen, "Graduate Education in Economics," *American Economic Review,* September 1953, Supplement, Part 2, p. 102.

[2] *Ibid.*, pp. 103–4.

[3] Sibley, *The Recruitment, Selection and Training of Social Scientists* (New York: Social Science Research Council, 1948), Bulletin 58, p. 5.

[4] Lee S. Green and Richard H. Leach, "Graduate Education and Research in Government in the South (Draft manuscript of a report of a commission established by the Southern Political Science Association, the Southern Public Administration Research Council, and the Southern Regional Education Board; Atlanta, Ga.: 1954), p. 23.

Other studies confirm that the methodological problem in political science is country-wide.[5]

The academic problems of international relations find their closest parallel, naturally enough, in the field with which it is most closely associated—political science. The latter has achieved the status of a recognized discipline in the United States, but by no means everywhere outside this country. In England, for example, A. H. Hanson writes that many universities have not yet started to consider the claims of political science as a separate discipline. Scholars there have not yet agreed on matters such as the extent to which it is vocational or cultural, the frontiers of the field, and the other subjects with which it should be associated. Some British university professors question the advisability of teaching so ill-defined a subject to immature undergraduates.[6]

The problem of the role of values and subjective preferences also is shared by political science and international relations. Hanson notes

the objections to political science that arise from its alleged lack of "objectivity." Much of the opposition to the improvement of its status springs from the opinion that it is hardly a "respectable" subject, because as soon as it ceases to be purely descriptive it becomes acutely controversial.[7]

In connection with this complaint, William Ebenstein reported,

In the preparatory commission which studied the creation of the International Political Science Association, an issue arose as to whether the term "political science" should continue to be used, on the ground that values as well as science were involved. In deciding to continue the term, the committee held that the essential characteristics of science—inductively obtained and systematically organized knowledge—are not a monopoly of any brand of scholarship and can be successfully applied to the study of government and politics.[8]

[5] James W. Fesler, *et al.*, "Goals for Political Science: A Discussion," *American Political Science Review*, December 1951, p. 266.

[6] Hanson, "Politics as a University Discipline," *Universities Quarterly*, November 1953, pp. 34–35.

[7] *Ibid.*, p. 40.

[8] Ebenstein, "Toward International Collaboration in Political Science: A

This is precisely the argument used by many in the South who defend the academic status of international relations.

Concluding the comparisons with political science, it should be remarked that both international relations and political science face the problem of delimitation of the area of competence. Professor Hanson, speaking of political science, states that:

The field is as wide as human society itself, and no aspect of it is fully intelligible without reference to at least some of its other aspects. . . . What are the frontiers of political science? The answer, I am certain, is that there are *no* clear frontiers. I believe that in the universities . . . it is a new integration, rather than a further fragmentation, of the 'social studies' disciplines that we need.[9]

These observations on the problems of political science are repeated in only slightly different form in a conference on the teaching of international relations:

This is not a territory that you can mark out on a map, the boundaries are not clear and sharp. . . . Perhaps it would be better if we did not give quite so much attention to "independent" disciplines, because I think they are becoming increasingly *inter*dependent.[10]

Similarly, in regard to this interdependence, Grayson Kirk observed that:

The point may be argued that . . . international politics does not become a separate discipline, but is merely a process of synthesizing the work of experts in the various fields. In one sense, however, while this method of study may differ in degree, it does not differ in kind from that followed in most of the other social studies. After a period of excessive specialization, the present trend is toward blurring the boundaries which have separated divisions of the social studies in the past. For example, the changing role of the state, particularly with respect to

Report on the Unesco Project, 'Methods in Political Science,'" *American Political Science Review*, December 1948, quoted in Marshall E. Dimock, *et al.*, *Goals for Political Science*, Report of the Committee for the Advancement of Teaching, American Political Science Association (New York: Dryden Press, 1951), pp. 18–19.

[9] Hanson, *op cit.*, pp. 37–38.

[10] Professors Frederick S. Dunn and Walter R. Sharp. Reproduced in Geoffrey L. Goodwin (ed.), *The University Teaching of International Relations* (New York: Macmillan Co., 1951), pp. 41–42.

economic matters, has created such a fusion of economics and politics that the economists and political scientists have more and more found that they were engaged upon converging lines of inquiry. Today, distinctions among the older divisions of the social studies are, in many cases, due less to separateness in subject-matter than to the fact that each is engaged in examining the same set of phenomena from a slightly different angle.[11]

This point of view is seconded in the name of political science:

We recommend that political scientists become increasingly concerned about the lessons they can learn from other social sciences, but that despite our attention to other areas, we still regard political science as a separate and distinct discipline. Our committee subscribes to the rule of subject-matter differentiation advocated by MacIver: "It is always the *focus* of interest which distinguishes one social science from another. . . . We should not think of the social sciences as dividing between them physically separate areas of reality. What distinguishes each from each is the selective interest."[12]

SOME VIEWS OF SOUTHERN TEACHERS

The similarities of the problems faced by international relations and other subjects may give perspective to the conflicting views of Southern teachers on the academic status of international relations. One extreme is represented by the teacher who asserted that although international relations "draws from history, political science, law, geography, economics, and other disciplines, it has its own independent approach, unique scope, and internal unity." The other extreme is exemplified by the statement of another teacher that "there is not enough subject matter in international relations to make it a separate field. If it is attempted, the result is only a mass of unrelated facts. It is best to train the student in a standard discipline so that he may see international relations through that perspective. Any social science could serve as a base to give a distinct methodological approach to international relations."

[11] Kirk, *The Study of International Relations in American Colleges and Universities* (New York: Council on Foreign Relations, 1947), pp. 11–12.

[12] *Goals for Political Science*, p. 131. The MacIver quotation is from R. M. MacIver and Charles H. Page, *Society: An Introductory Analysis* (New York: Rinehart & Co., 1949), p. v.

Those who subscribe to the latter view generally argue that history, political science, economics, or some other social science gives sufficient understanding of international relations. On the other hand, some who share this view agree that often international relations is thrown in only as an afterthought by the other disciplines, and that the concern of these disciplines for international relations is more an ideal than a reality.

METHODOLOGY

Those who consider international relations as a subject for separate study generally concede that it has no specific methodology of its own. They would agree with Professor Sharp that:

International Relations is a legitimate *field* for study. It does not necessarily have any special *method* of its own, it draws for its methods and techniques of study from a great many fields that are perhaps better established than it is.[13]

It should be noted that the concession of lack of method is, for the defenders of international relations, not an apology. Probably most of the defenders in the South would agree that international relations does not need its own methodology. It can use the methodologies of other social science disciplines in the focus of its own subject matter.

These considerations suggest that methodology in international relations should be discussed in connection with methodology in the social sciences in general. There may be considerable agreement that while no unique methodology of international relations has been evolved,

using the example of Galileo and astronomy . . . where there is a set of problems there is, in effect, a discipline: the methods are developed to solve the problems, and in time people begin to analyze the methods and develop the theories.[14]

13 Geoffrey L. Goodwin (ed.), *The University Teaching of International Relations* (Oxford: B. H. Blackwell, Ltd., 1951), p. 42.

14 The Brookings Institution, The International Studies Group, "Report on a Conference on the Teaching of International Relations," held at Charlottesville, Va., January 26–28, 1950, p. 22.

This statement points the way to a consideration of method as a common fund of procedures to which all the various aspects, or "disciplines," in the social sciences (and, indeed, natural sciences) have contributed in the process of delving into the problems that constitute their special field of interest. In these terms it would seem both proper and necessary that there be generous borrowing from this common store of investigative procedures. Moreover, if problems precede and often stimulate a search for means to solve them, then it may be expected that international relations is as capable of making methodological contributions as other fields of specialization.

CONCEPTUALIZATION

Whatever the consequences for methodology, the great majority of those interviewed expressed the belief that conceptualization and theoretical structure constitute the greatest need of international relations as a field of study. Many would agree with one teacher's opinion that the lack of conceptualization is one of the main causes for the controversies over the place of international relations in the curriculum.

Grayson Kirk also was concerned with the unprecise structure of international relations when he declared that "one must ask seriously if there is such a thing as international relations."[15] His answer was that:

it is necessary to consider just what a student of international relations attempts to do. His objectives are many and varied but most of them can be grouped under five main headings. These are: (1) analysis of the various forces which influence the foreign policies of the principal states of the world; (2) critical examination of the method which states use to carry on their business with each other, and the instrumentalities which they have established for that purpose; (3) assessment of contemporary economic, political and legal relations among states, and the trends which they reveal; (4) study of the means by which conflicts among states may be adjusted; and (5) consideration of the legal and moral principles which should govern intercourse among nations. . . . The

[15] Kirk, *op. cit.*, p. 8.

focus must be on intergovernmental relations and all things which affect them.[16]

This description of the interests of the student of international relations specifies that the essence of the subject is political. As was noted earlier, this view is supported by the great majority of those interviewed, as well as in relevant writings. Indeed, there are many who use the terms "international relations" and "international politics" interchangeably. This usage sometimes provokes dissent; the area of disagreement would be reduced, said one Southern teacher, if international relations were understood as "politics in the Aristotelian sense, embracing law, organization, ideology and theory."

ACADEMIC AFFILIATION WITH POLITICAL SCIENCE

In any case, the primary role of politics in international relations makes it appropriate at this point to discuss its academic connection with political science. This has been a subject of considerable concern, underlined by the *Goals* study which devoted a special chapter to the teaching of international relations. The authors were emphatic in their conclusions that international relations is inseparable from political science:

Withdraw them [core subjects in international relations] from the political science department and one of two things will happen: either there will be a costly and stultifying duplication, or the political science department will be left in a weakened condition, stripped of what is most essential in its personnel and structure.[17]

If the proposition of such a close relationship is accepted, it is understandable that the authors of *Goals* deprecate any tendencies toward the establishment of independent departments of international relations. This position is supported by a good number of teachers interviewed, including both those actually teaching international relations and those in other fields. The consensus of this group is represented by a teacher of compara-

[16] *Ibid.*, pp. 8–9.
[17] *Goals for Political Science,* p. 66.

tive government who said that it was unhealthy to distinguish between international relations and political science because it might lead to a dissipation of energy. But the same teacher revealed the problematic nature of this prescription by adding: "Of course, international relations permits one to do things which standard disciplines won't allow."

The difficulties attending curricular organization and departmental jurisdiction, then, seem to raise perhaps more important practical issues than those connected with the question of whether or not international relations is or can be separate from political science. While there is general agreement that the core is political, there is also general agreement that international relations must be studied on an interdisciplinary basis. The latter consensus is used as the chief argument for the establishment of independent departments of international relations or interdepartmental committees which would de-emphasize traditional departmental requirements in favor of an interdisciplinary approach. Both critics and advocates of the interdisciplinary approach are inclined to subscribe to the view that the movement to make international relations a distinct discipline gains little of its momentum from the conviction that it is uniquely different from any other discipline. The momentum is gained, rather, from the desire to transcend existing departmental restrictions and requirements so that the student may devote adequate time to the several disciplines which bear on his subject, and engage in more intensive application of the disciplines to the specific problems of international relations.

In the ordinary international relations program, the amount of time spent in the study of history and economics and other social sciences often equals or exceeds the time spent in political science courses. Again and again during the interview program, it was stated that the international relations student must, of course, have certain history and economics courses—geography and the social sciences were mentioned less often—whereas many of those interviewed felt either that political science does not need to reach into other fields to so great an extent or conceded that, theoretically, courses in other fields are just as desirable for political science students as for international relations students. The difference is that in international relations the interdisciplinary idea is accepted as a matter of course.

In passing, it may be noted that there were several teachers in various social science fields who remarked during the course of the interviews that international relations is uniquely suited to forward the objective of closer interdisciplinary cooperation. One teacher participating in a formal international relations program put it thus: "We do not look upon ourselves as a further academic fragmentation but as a reintegration."

One advocate of a separate international relations department explained: "The student of international affairs can no longer be confined within the limits of the older disciplines because the very nature of the subject requires a broader and an integrative approach. Only by redefining the older disciplines in the broadest terms so that each includes all the others could this situation be avoided." Perhaps there would be agreement that if all the social science disciplines are examining different aspects of the same phenomena, then such a redefinition has—on the level of theory—already taken place. Where the ecumenical view of the social sciences prevails in practice as well as in theory, there international relations can flourish under whatever administrative arrangement there may be for the distinguishing of the disciplines. Where such a view is not held, or is held in theory only, many would contend that there will be continued pressure on the part of international relations advocates to escape the bonds of departmental restrictions and to set up departments of their own.

Whatever the interdisciplinary needs of international relations, the experience gained from the interviews for this survey supports the proposition made at the beginning of this discussion —that the core of international relations is political and that all effort in this field must culminate in political analysis. As such, international relations may be considered a branch of political science. But, in the eyes of many, international relations probably will remain in practice something different from political science in those institutions that insist that a student of politics confine his study almost entirely to the political science department.

Development and Future Plans of International Relations Programs

Regardless of the disciplinary status of international relations, it has become established as a course subject or program of study in a number of Southern colleges and universities, especially in those offering graduate degrees. The questionnaires were prepared on the assumption that this was the prevailing situation, without challenging the theoretical implications.

In one section of the questionnaire, institutions in Group I (those offering graduate programs leading to at least a master's degree in political science) and Group II (those with undergraduate majors in political science) were queried concerning the number of years their courses or programs in international relations had been in existence; how the formal programs, if any, came to be established; and what changes in offerings had been made since 1945. All institutions in the survey were asked what future plans for changing the present offerings might be.

NUMBER OF YEARS INTERNATIONAL RELATIONS PROGRAMS OR COURSES HAVE BEEN ESTABLISHED

The percentages in Table 4 indicate certain trends, although they are not based on enough cases to be definitive. The figures indicate that nearly half the Group I respondents reported programs or courses in existence twenty-one years or more at the time of the survey. This does not, of course, necessarily imply that the offerings have been in their present form that long. Approximately 30 percent of the programs reported by Group I schools were begun six to ten years before the survey, or in the

TABLE 4

NUMBER OF YEARS INTERNATIONAL RELATIONS COURSES OR PROGRAMS
HAVE BEEN IN EXISTENCE IN GROUP I AND GROUP II INSTITUTIONS

NO. OF YEARS IN EXISTENCE	GROUP I, GRADUATE LEVEL		GROUP I, UNDERGRADUATE LEVEL		GROUP II	
	No.	Percent of Responding Schools (*N = 19*)	No.	Percent of Responding Schools (*N = 28*)	No.	Percent of Responding Schools (*N = 49*)
0–5..................	1	5	2	7	8	16
6–10.................	6	32	8	29	15	31
11–15................	1	5	0	0	10	20
16–20................	3	16	5	18	3	6
21 or more...........	8	42	13	46	13	27
No answer...........	13	....	4	....	22	....
Total.............	32	100	32	100	71	100

period immediately following World War II. Only a few were established during the war years or very recently.

Programs in Group II colleges seem generally to have been in existence for a much shorter time than those in Group I: only a third were begun before World War II, in contrast to two thirds of those in Group I; a fifth were established during the war period, and nearly half since the war. World War II obviously had some effect upon the establishment of courses in both categories of institutions, but the effect upon Group II was greater, since programs already were in existence on most Group I campuses.

REASONS FOR ESTABLISHMENT OF FORMAL
INTERNATIONAL RELATIONS PROGRAMS

The question concerning the reasons for the establishment of formal programs in Group I and Group II institutions produced some information about the number of these formal programs, as shown in Table 5.

Respondents gave an average of about two reasons each for the establishment of international relations programs; thus, the total number of reasons shown in Table 6 is about twice the number of respondents.

TABLE 5

RESPONSE OF GROUP I AND GROUP II INSTITUTIONS TO QUESTION ABOUT
ESTABLISHMENT OF FORMAL INTERNATIONAL RELATIONS PROGRAMS

RESPONSE TO QUESTION	NO. OF INSTITUTIONS		
	Group I, Graduate Level	Group I, Undergraduate Level	Group II
Gave reasons for establishment of program....................	8	12	22
Specified no formal program.......	5	8	13
No response....................	19	12	36
Total.....................	32	32	71

Trends were similar for all groups, although differing some-what in degree. Availability of faculty members specializing in international relations was listed most frequently, with result of a curriculum study and student demand also of importance. Research opportunities were understandably more important in Group I, especially in the graduate schools. Student demand seems to have been more important in the undergraduate col-

TABLE 6

REASONS GIVEN FOR ESTABLISHMENT OF FORMAL PROGRAMS IN
INTERNATIONAL RELATIONS IN GROUP I AND GROUP II INSTITUTIONS

TYPE OF REASON GIVEN	FREQUENCY OF RESPONSE					
	Group I, Graduate Level		Group I, Undergraduate Level		Group II	
	No.	Percent	No.	Percent	No.	Percent
Result of a curriculum study..............	4	22	9	29	11	27
Faculty specialties	7	39	10	32	14	35
Student demand........	3	17	7	23	12	30
Research opportunities of the area.............	3	17	3	10	2	5
Assigned grants.........	1	5	1	3	1	3
Other................	0	0	1*	3	0	0
Total................	18	100	31	100	40	100

*Idea suggested by alumni of the school.

leges. This may be because a graduate student is normally interested in a certain specialty and applies only to schools which already have programs in that field, whereas undergraduates generally pay less attention to specialized programs when choosing a college, but may express a wish for certain subjects as their curiosity is stimulated.

Assigned grants apparently played an almost negligible part in the establishment of programs. If curriculum study, faculty specialties, and research opportunities may be taken together as aspects of faculty interest, it would seem that faculty members have been the primary instigators for the development of international relations programs. This was perhaps to be expected; but the overwhelming predominance of faculty initiative and the almost total absence of outside pressures are interesting points.

CHANGES IN INTERNATIONAL RELATIONS OFFERINGS

Many of the responses to a question regarding changes in offerings since 1945 indicated merely that some change had occurred (see Table 7 for a summary of replies from Group I and II institutions). In some cases, however, there was a description of the change, suggesting whether addition or subtraction of facilities was involved, as shown in Table 8.

Apparently, most of the changes have involved increases in the

TABLE 7

CHANGES IN INTERNATIONAL RELATIONS OFFERINGS SINCE 1945
IN GROUP I AND GROUP II INSTITUTIONS

RESPONSE	NO. OF INSTITUTIONS		
	Group I, Graduate Level	Group I, Undergraduate Level	Group II
Reported changes...............	21	26	35
Reported no change..............	0	2	18
No answer.....................	11	4	18
Total......................	32	32	71

TABLE 8

KINDS OF CHANGES IN INTERNATIONAL RELATIONS OFFERINGS SINCE 1945 IN GROUP I AND GROUP II INSTITUTIONS

NO. OF INSTITUTIONS REPORTING

TYPE OF CHANGE	Group I, Graduate Level				Group I, Undergraduate Level				Group II			
	Change	Increase	Decrease	Total	Change	Increase	Decrease	Total	Change	Increase	Decrease	Total
Degrees offered	0	2	0	2	0	1	0	1	0	1	0	1
Course offerings	8	10	0	18	9	15	0	24	4	26	0	30
Field work opportunities	2	2	0	4	3	3	0	6	2	0	0	2
Number and specialties of faculty	7	11	0	18	6	15	0	21	6	11	0	17
Number, interests, and demands of students	2	7	1	10	5	9	1	15	2	8	1	11
Other*	1	2	0	3	1	1	0	2	0	0	0	0

*Other changes in Group I institutions included: At the graduate level, (a) change in administrative plans; (b) increase in number of foreign students and foreign relations study groups; (c) increase in appropriations and funds for scholarships and fuller use of government programs for visiting professors and students. At the undergraduate level, (a) change in administrative plans; (b) increase in appropriations.

number of courses and the number and specialties of faculty members. Next in importance has been a change in the interests and demands of students. Twenty-four institutions indicated greater student interest. Only three reported a decrease, and one of these was attributed to state requirements for teacher certification. There were few indications of changes in degrees offered, in field work opportunities, or in other matters relevant to offerings in international relations.

The almost unanimous reports of heightened student interest contrast sharply with the complaints of student apathy noted in the interviews. The discrepancy may be explained at least in part by the nature of the inquiry. In the questionnaires, "interest" appears to have been judged statistically, by such criteria as the number of students registering for courses in the subject. In the interviews, the reports of apathy came from teachers of courses who deplored the reluctance of students to indulge in spirited classroom debate.

An objective for future investigation is here suggested. What constitutes "interest," or how is it to be measured? In the 1930's, some students argued vociferously the problem of good and evil in international relations; but it must be remembered that the majority remained cynically silent. Today the problem is construed as not one of good and evil, but as one of "we" and "they." Yet more students apparently seek knowledge of the subject. It may be that one generation sought desperately for a point of view, while the next looks for information to implement action based upon a point of view which appears established beyond challenge.

FUTURE PLANS FOR CHANGING OFFERINGS IN INTERNATIONAL RELATIONS

All the institutions in the survey were asked to indicate their future plans for enlarging or changing their programs or courses in international relations. While there was not an unusually high proportion failing to answer this question, there was a rather marked tendency to answer the question negatively (see Table 9). This was especially true in Groups II and III, where approximately 70 percent of the replies specified that no changes were being planned. At the other end of the scale were the graduate divisions of Group I; 82 percent of those responding were planning changes.

TABLE 9

FUTURE PLANS OF SOUTHERN INSTITUTIONS FOR CHANGING PRESENT
OFFERINGS IN INTERNATIONAL RELATIONS

RESPONSE	NO. OF INSTITUTIONS				
	Group I, Graduate Level	Group I, Under-graduate Level	Group II	Group III	Group IV
Reported plans for change..	14	16	17	17	4
Reported no plans for change	3	10	38	43	5
No answer...............	15	6	16	16	3
Total...............	32	32	71	76	12

As shown in Table 10, the kinds of changes under consideration varied considerably, but in all groups the greatest number of plans were being made for changes in the courses offered, and, in most cases, for the addition of a new course or courses. The emphasis on the addition of courses in future plans was particularly strong in the smaller colleges.

The next most frequently mentioned plan was for changes in or additions to the faculty. Most institutions indicating a change in faculty composition stated the intention of adding one or two new faculty members in the near future.

Among the Group I graduate divisions, about a third of those answering the question planned to offer a new degree in the near future. Few changes in field work opportunities were being considered by the responding schools. A scattering of other types of changes were being planned, including the establishment of whole new curricula, the initiation of workshops, new emphasis on area studies and area contacts, the development of new ad-

TABLE 10

KINDS OF CHANGES IN INTERNATIONAL RELATIONS OFFERINGS PLANNED BY SOUTHERN INSTITUTIONS

TYPE OF CHANGE	Group I, Graduate Level			Group I, Undergraduate Level			Group II			Group III			Group IV		
	Change	Increase	Total	Change	Increase	Total	Change	Increase	Total	Change	Increase	Total	Change	Increase	Total
Degrees offered	0	5	5	0	1	1	0	2	2	0	2	2	0	0	0
Courses offered	2	5	7	1	7	8	1	11	12	3	11	14	1	2	3
Field work opportunities	1	2	3	0	3	3	1	0	1	0	0	0	0	0	0
Composition of faculty	3	3	6	1	5	6	0	3	3	1	6	7	0	1	1
Other*	2	4	6	2	5	7	0	3	3	1	4	5	0	0	0

*Group I, Graduate.—(a) Curriculum change possibly leading to area program; (b) curriculum change; (c) establishment of school of international commerce and diplomacy; (d) establishment of special program in international relations; (e) bringing officials of foreign governments to campus; (f) new administrative organization of international affairs program.

Group I, Undergraduate Level.—(a) Possible re-establishment of Slavic studies; (b) curriculum increases in Asian area work; (c) curriculum changes; (d) establishment of school of international commerce and diplomacy; (e) establishment of special program; (f) development of Russian and East European interdepartmental program; (g) possible new administrative organization of international affairs program.

Group II.—(a) Summer workshop in international relations for adult women; (b) more foreign language because of government examinations; (c) establishment of chapter of International Relations Club.

Group III.—(a) Emphasis upon each student's having an experience in a culture other than his own; (b) possible offering of American Foundation for Political Education course in world politics as an adult education course; (c) establishment of a ten-week seminar, as a degree requirement for adult education, with Ford Foundation films and pamphlets, on current problem-areas of the earth; (d) requirement that all prospective social studies teachers take a course in geography of the United States and neighboring lands; (e) incorporation of the departments of geography and of sociology into the department of social studies.

ministrative arrangements, and the greater utilization of foreign personnel.

Academic Offerings

This section is concerned, first, with institutional responses to questions about the departments that teach international relations and related subjects; the disciplines wherein major emphasis upon subject matter within this field may be obtained; the statement of institutions as to whether *formal* emphasis may be given to the field of international relations by a student wishing to specialize; those disciplines considered as supporting to the field wherein major emphasis may be obtained; and related matters.

Second, the section presents a summary of the characteristics of courses listed by responding institutions as "wholly or partly designed to give the student an understanding of international relations."

Last, this section lists the required texts and readings used most often in the principal course or courses in international relations, as reported by the responding schools.

ACADEMIC DEPARTMENTS

Responding institutions listed a total of 697 academic departments as offering courses closely related to international relations, an average of nearly four different departments per institution. Of the total number of departments, Group I, graduate and undergraduate levels, reported 39 percent of the 697 departments; Group II, 31 percent; Group III, 25 percent; and Group IV, 5 percent. The undergraduate divisions of Group I reported, on the average, more departments than the other groups, and were followed by the other groups in the following order: Group I graduate divisions, Group II, Group IV, and Group III. The range was from an average of five departments for Group I undergraduate level to an average of two departments for Group III.

Table 11 presents the relative frequency of listing of various

TABLE 11

DISTRIBUTION OF DEPARTMENTS OFFERING COURSES CLOSELY RELATED TO INTERNATIONAL RELATIONS

Department Offering Courses Closely Related to International Relations	Group I, Graduate Level (%)	Group I, Undergraduate Level (%)	Group II (%)	Group III (%)	Group IV (%)	All Groups Combined (%)
Total number of departments listed..	*108*	*160*	*218*	*177*	*34*	*697*
Political science..........	21	18	15	11	6	15
History..........	21	16	17	23	9	19
History and political science......	1	2	10	6	9	5
Subtotal, political science and history..........	43	36	42	40	24	39
Economics and business administration..........	25	22	18	13	20	19
Geography..........	8	12	5	8	3	8
Social studies..........	0	0	6	17	12	7
Sociology and anthropology......	8	11	6	5	9	7
Foreign languages..........	4	4	8	6	3	6
Other*..........	12	15	15	11	29	14
Total..........	100	100	100	100	100	100

*Includes psychology, humanities, law, etc.

departments by the different groups of institutions. A subtotal percentage is given for political science and history departments because there were many *combined* political science and history departments in the smaller colleges. It should be noted that the social studies departments in Groups II, III, and IV institutions also may encompass history and political science, or may comprise only other social studies fields.

Looking at the last column of Table 11, one might summarize the emphasis given various departments by Southern schools: The departments mentioned clearly with the greatest frequency are political science, history, and economics. On the basis of the percentages, there is little distinction in the emphasis given these three fields. Social studies generally seems to be considered next in importance, for when social studies departments and departments of sociology and/or anthropology are grouped together, they represent about 14 percent of the total list. Next comes geography; then foreign languages; and then a scattering of many other disciplines, including psychology, philosophy, law, religion, and so on.

Certain trends may be observed in comparing the lists given by the larger universities with those returned by smaller or technical institutions. In Groups III and IV, political science departments were listed with less frequency, doubtless because there are fewer separate departments of political science in those schools. On the other hand among the smaller colleges, larger percentages appear for departments of history and political science combined and for departments of social studies. The position of economics remained consistent throughout all groups of institutions.

The greatest deviation from the general trends, aside from the decrease of separate departments of political science and the increase in departments combining disciplines among the smaller and technical colleges, was the high percentage of departments falling in the "Other" category for Group IV, the technical institutions. This deviation can be accounted for largely by the frequent listing of military science departments by colleges in that group.

DEPARTMENT OFFERING GREATEST PORTION
OF WORK IN INTERNATIONAL RELATIONS

Questions concerning the department offering the greatest portion of the work in international relations within the institution were directed to institutions in Groups I and II only. Table 12 presents the responses of these groups, separating the answers that listed one discipline wherein the greatest portion of work was offered from those that listed more than one. The "several disciplines" category includes both those listing two disciplines in two separate departments and those where one department encompassed the work given in several disciplines.

The most striking point apparent from Table 12 is the tendency for Group I universities in both graduate and undergraduate divisions to list a single discipline or department as offering the major portion of its courses related to international relations; and for Group II institutions to list a multidisciplinary department or several departments (usually only two) as collectively offering the major portion of work. This point would be even more apparent

TABLE 12

DEPARTMENT OFFERING THE GREATEST PORTION OF WORK IN
INTERNATIONAL RELATIONS, GROUP I AND GROUP II INSTITUTIONS

Department(s)	Group I, Graduate Level (%)	Group I, Undergraduate Level (%)	Group II (%)
Number of institutions	32	32	71
One discipline:			
Political science	38	50	30
Other	6	6	7
Several disciplines:			
Political science-history	19	16	35
Others	9	22	22
No answer	28	6	6
Total	100	100	100

were it not for the large proportion of "no answer" institutions in the Group I graduate-level category. Actually, more than half of the *answering* universities in the Group I graduate-level category reported the political science department as the single one where the major portion of work in the field was offered. There is in these figures perhaps an indication of greater specialization among the Group I institutions, at both graduate and undergraduate levels, and a suggestion that work in the field in Group II colleges tends to be more general, or at least more dispersed among various academic disciplines.

Next to political science, the history department was mentioned with the greatest frequency as a department where major emphasis was given. Under the "several disciplines" category, where combinations other than history–political science were grouped under "Others," departments of economics and of social studies were mentioned frequently; that is, there were instances where economics was mentioned in combination with either political science or history or both, and instances where the social studies department, alone or with others, was listed.

Departments listed as concerned with major emphasis, but not as themselves offering a major portion of the work, were the following: area studies, business administration, economics, English, geography, history, journalism, languages, law, philosophy, political science, psychology, religion, and sociology and anthropology. The fields are listed alphabetically, with no indication of the frequency with which each field was mentioned, because there were many institutions that failed to answer the question regarding supporting departments. Indications of relative importance in terms of frequency mentioned, therefore, would be misleading.

FORMAL EMPHASIS; DEGREES

Because information concerning administrative arrangements for programs with formal emphasis on international relations study was given rather inconsistently, and because very few institutions indicated a special title for these formal programs, the tabulation can show only the presence or absence of a program with such formal emphasis. Table 13 indicates that formal emphasis was checked as available in half or nearly half the institutions in Group I at both the graduate and undergraduate levels,

TABLE 13

PERCENTAGE OF INSTITUTIONS IN GROUPS I AND II OFFERING
FORMAL EMPHASIS IN INTERNATIONAL RELATIONS

Offering	Group I, Graduate Level (%)	Group I, Undergraduate Level (%)	Group II (%)
Number of institutions............	*32*	*32*	*71*
Formal emphasis.................	44	50	32
No formal emphasis..............	28	44	62
No answer....................	28	6	6
Total......................	100	100	100

and in approximately one third of the institutions in Group II. Although only a little over one fourth of the Group I institutions indicated specifically that there was *no* formal emphasis at the graduate level, the fact that all but one of the "no answer" institutions in this group returned an undergraduate but not a graduate questionnaire suggests strongly that they had no formal graduate programs.

Among the fourteen Group I institutions offering graduate-level work and indicating that formal emphasis was available, five, or about one third, reported that the doctor of philosophy degree was given in the department offering the major portion of work. Special degrees indicated in Group I institutions, aside from the Ph.D.,[18] were the M.A. in Foreign Affairs (the major department) from the University of Virginia, and the Certificate in International Affairs, given in addition to the B.A., at Tulane Univer-

[18] Note that the original criterion for placing a school in Group I was the offering of a master's degree in political science. Hence, the master's degree with a major in political science is not considered as "special" here.

sity. Among the Group II colleges, the B.A. in International Affairs at Sweet Briar and the B.A. in International Relations at Goucher were of special note. Both of these programs, it may be noted incidentally, were administered by committees drawn from several disciplines, including political science, history, and economics.

COURSES

Certain problems were encountered in the tabulation of courses listed by responding institutions as "wholly or partly designed to give the student an understanding of international relations." The complexity of the question about courses itself and the variety in possible responses as to title of course, length of course (quarter, semester, year), and frequency of course offering (every year, more frequently, or less frequently) made it difficult to gather the data into usable and comparable form.

In the first place, it was necessary that some method be devised for classifying the various course titles, for even courses obviously very similar in content had varying titles. An initial attempt to deal with the courses almost title by title left the researchers with over two hundred categories, and even these were not nearly sufficient to cover the multitude of minor variations. As a result, pages of qualifications and explanations would have been necessary in order for the reader to understand where a course with a particular title might be classified. Ultimately, the researchers abandoned the attempt to present a detailed or highly refined system of course classification and instead adopted forty-eight general classifications,[19] with the following purposes in mind:

1. That the general title of each course group be sufficiently descriptive so that the reader would have little difficulty in surmising most of the individual course titles that might be included in that category;

2. That the courses dealing specifically with international mat-

---

[19] A complete list of the forty-eight categories used in the final tabulation of courses is given in Tables 18 and 19 on pp. 78–81.

ters be grouped separately, wherever possible, from other courses in each discipline;

3. That course groupings avoid crossing disciplinary lines so that it might be possible for further groupings to be made of the categories into larger disciplinary classifications, i.e., political science, history, economics, geography, social science, humanities, and miscellaneous; and

4. That consideration be given, where possible, to setting up separate categories for different areas of the world so that Latin America, Europe, and Asia, as a minimum, might be summarized across disciplinary lines.

A second difficulty in compiling data that could give a reasonably accurate picture of the quantity of work being offered by the various institutions in the fields listed above was created by the almost infinite variety in the quantity value that could be assigned to any one course when both length and frequency of offering were taken into account. For example, a course one quarter in length could be offered twice a year, every other year, and so on. Similarly, a semester course could be offered twice yearly, or during the summer only, or infrequently. The problem was resolved by dropping from final tabulations consideration of the frequency with which a course was offered. This seemed justified in view of the fact that the largest number of courses (69 percent) was offered on a yearly basis (see Table 14). Very few courses were offered less frequently than every other year. Nevertheless, this method of presentation does introduce a slight distortion, for the group totals represent a few more hours of work than the number actually offered during one academic year. It may be noted, however, that in only one instance, the political science courses in Group III, did the percentage of courses offered yearly or more often fall below 50 percent.

The final assessment of the quantities of work given in the various fields was based on a transformation of the *length* of the course into the number of hours ordinarily assigned as credit for a course of that length, that is, one quarter equals two hours, one

TABLE 14

COURSES CONTRIBUTING TO INTERNATIONAL RELATIONS STUDY,* OFFERED YEARLY OR MORE FREQUENTLY, BY DISCIPLINE, AS REPORTED BY EACH GROUP

Key: N = Number of courses
%A = percent offered yearly or more frequently

DISCIPLINE	GROUP I		GROUP II		GROUP III		GROUP IV		ALL GROUPS	
	N	%A	N	%A	N	%A	N	%A	N	%A
Political science	271	79	216	52	94	48	14	64	595	64
History	155	69	200	57	201	63	21	100	577	64
Economics	109	79	59	54	38	61	7	71	213	69
Geography	90	91	63	73	48	69	4	100	205	81
Social studies	36	83	29	66	28	75	7	100	100	77
Humanities and miscellaneous	20	95	48	85	48	81	8	100	124	86
All disciplines	681	79	615	59	457	63	61	89	1,814	69

*Total number of courses equal 2,014. This represents 7,016 hours of work, and further tabulation and discussion of course work will be based on hours, rather than courses, as the unit. Length of the courses varied from one quarter to a full year, with all intermediate variations possible. Total number of courses upon which percentages in this table were based is 1,814, or 90 percent of all courses listed by all schools. Information concerning the frequency of offering the course was not given by responding institutions in the other 10 percent of the cases.

semester equals three hours, two quarters equals four hours, and one year equals six hours.

References to Group I schools in this section on courses include graduate and undergraduate courses together. This change in procedure was made because many courses, listed in either the undergraduate or graduate forms of the returned questionnaires, were offered to *both* graduate and undergraduate students. In a separate consideration of Group I, tabulation and discussion of the proportion of courses offered to undergraduates only, to graduates only, and to both are given (see Table 17, page 58).

GENERAL CHARACTERISTICS OF COURSE WORK LISTED

A total of 7,016 hours of work "wholly or partly designed to give a student an understanding of international relations" was reported by the 191 responding institutions, an average of about 37 hours per institution. Table 15 shows the proportion of course hours contributed by each group, and the proportion of all institutions represented by each group. It should be emphasized that the Group I figure contains offerings listed in the graduate as well as the undergraduate returned questionnaires.

The distribution of concentration in each discipline may be observed by reference to the last column in Table 16. It is interesting to note that, while economics was given almost equal at-

TABLE 15

PROPORTION OF ANSWERING INSTITUTIONS IN
EACH GROUP AND PROPORTION OF HOURS OF
COURSE WORK REPORTED BY
EACH GROUP

Group	Percentage of Institutions (N = 191)	Percentage of Course Hours (N = 7,016)
Group I.............	17	41
Group II............	37	31
Group III...........	40	25
Group IV...........	6	3
Total...........	100	100

TABLE 16

DISTRIBUTION OF COURSE HOURS AMONG DISCIPLINES,
BY INSTITUTIONAL GROUPINGS

DISCIPLINE	PERCENTAGE OF HOURS OF COURSE WORK				
	Group I	Group II	Group III	Group IV	All Groups
Political science............	38	34	19	17	31
History..................	27	36	50	36	36
Economics...............	16	8	7	11	11
Geography...............	11	8	9	7	10
Social science.............	5	5	5	13	5
Humanities and miscellaneous...........	3	9	10	16	7
Total...............	100	100	100	100	100

tention with political science and history in the lists of departments or disciplines participating in international relations study
(see above sections), the amount of course work listed in economics was far less for all four groups than the amount of work
listed in political science or history. The role of geography seems
different, too, in the report on course work from its role in questions on departmental participation. While that role was rather
unimportant in the lists of departments, it assumed a position
nearly as important as that of economics in the listing of courses.

One of the most interesting features of the responses to the
question on course offerings was the shift in emphasis given the
various disciplines, which is evidenced as Group I is compared
with Groups II, III, and IV (Table 16). The proportion of course
hours drawn from history departments was far greater in the other
three groups, and in particular in Group III, than in Group I.
Groups I and II drew upon a large proportion of political science
courses while Groups III and IV did not. It is apparent also that
the smaller colleges drew to a greater degree than the larger institutions upon a wide range of course offerings as the respondents
considered what was available relative to international relations
in their institutions. This is clear from reference to the increase
in percentage of offerings drawn from the social sciences and hu-

manities and miscellaneous categories in the smaller and technical schools (Groups II, III, and IV) as compared with those in Group I.

LEVEL OF OFFERINGS IN GROUP I INSTITUTIONS

It will be seen from Table 17 that a high percentage of the work offered in Group I institutions was available to both graduates and undergraduates. In most disciplines the work exclusively for students on one level was about evenly balanced between grad-

TABLE 17

PERCENTAGE OF HOURS OF COURSE WORK OFFERED IN EACH DISCIPLINE TO UNDERGRADUATES, GRADUATES, AND BOTH, AS REPORTED BY INSTITUTIONS IN GROUP I

DISCIPLINE	PERCENTAGE OF COURSE HOURS OFFERED			
	Exclusively to Undergraduates	Exclusively to Graduates	To Both	Total
Political science...........	23	24	53	100
History...................	29	21	50	100
Economics................	24	21	55	100
Geography...............	39	10	51	100
Social science.............	27	32	41	100
Humanities and miscellaneous...........	32	7	61	100
All fields................	*27*	*21*	*52*	*100*

uate and undergraduate offerings. There was a heavy preponderance of undergraduate offerings, however, in geography and in the humanities and miscellaneous category; but so few courses were reported in the latter areas that the percentage figures cannot be considered too reliable an indication.

Summary

The status of international relations as a discipline is challenged by criticisms that it has no central core or coherent methodology. Most teachers seem agreed that conceptualization and theoretical structure are the greatest needs of international relations as a field of study. Although there is strong opinion that international relations is so closely related to political science as perhaps to be inseparable, there is widespread agreement that it must be studied on an interdisciplinary basis. In existing international relations programs, the time spent in history, economics, and other social sciences often equals or exceeds the time spent in political science.

Tables presented in this chapter indicate that:

1. International relations programs or courses have been in existence somewhat longer in Group I than in Group II institutions.

2. Faculty specialties were listed most frequently as a reason for the establishment of formal international relations programs.

3. Most of the changes made since 1945 have involved increases in number of courses or in number of faculty specialties.

4. Relatively few changes in international relations offerings were contemplated at the time of the survey.

5. An average of nearly four departments was listed as offering courses closely related to international relations.

6. The major portion of international relations work tended to be offered in a single discipline in Group I institutions, but in a multidisciplinary department or in more than one department collectively in Group II institutions.

7. Formal emphasis in international relations was reported available in one half or nearly one half of the Group I institutions and about one third of those in Group II.

8. Slightly under a third of the total courses related to international relations in all institutions were in political science; however, Groups III and IV listed more such courses in history than in political science, and all except Group I listed history as contributing more hours of course work than political science.

9. Of the hours offered in Group I institutions, about half were for both graduates and undergraduates and the remainder about equally divided between offerings exclusively for each group.

4

Courses for the Specialist

W<small>HY MUST THE</small> student of international relations go beyond the confines of the political science department? To answer
this question, it is necessary to establish what the student seeks to
do. Based on the interviews for this survey, as well as on the writings of international relations teachers outside the South, some
general statements may be made. The purpose of the international relations student is to examine the factors operative in
dealings between sovereign states, the objectives arising within
this complex of factors, the instruments used to achieve the objectives, and the norms and rules by which it is sought to harmonize
the objectives or to resolve conflicting objectives. He will want to
study what the past discloses about all these matters, and therefore history is of basic importance. The factors and objectives run
the gamut of phenomena in the province of the social sciences;
hence, he must explore economics, sociology, and other fields in
the social sciences, as well as politics. Moreover, since human be-
ings are the common denominator of the social sciences, the student of international relations cannot do without the insights
which literature, art, and the other humanities provide. The instruments themselves are political, economic, legal, military, psy-
chological, and ideological. And the norms are political, legal, and
philosophical.

Admittedly, this is a large order. Yet does it differ greatly from
a standard major in political science, for example? Is not the
political scientist faced with an equally formidable complex, with
some variations in emphasis? It might be argued that international relations, spanning the world, involves a greater mass of

data than does political science and that the latter is thus better able to concentrate on the concrete and avoid generalities. But politics also spans the world, and the fact that political scientists have traditionally concentrated on the country or countries about which they teach does not reduce the amount of empirical political data to be encompassed.

In any case, it is clear that both political science and international relations have more to offer than the student—graduate or undergraduate—can hope to absorb. The best they can do is give each student insight into their methods of research, theory, instruments, and norms and then help him to explore the massive field of factors in the light of his own talents and interests. With these aims in mind, it is perhaps appropriate now to give some consideration to the fields which have been recommended or suggested as those the international relations student should or may cover.

Fields To Be Covered

First, it may be useful to have an overview of what these fields are considered to be. Almost everyone interviewed in the course of the survey was asked his opinion concerning the subject matter which international relations ought to comprise. Following is a list of the subjects mentioned. They are grouped together by field, with the politics, government, and law subjects listed first, followed by those in history, economics, geography, sociology, anthropology, humanities, and area study. The order of the list does not carry with it any implication concerning the number of times each field was mentioned, as many interviewees gave incomplete answers and it was evident that these instructors simply assumed certain subjects ought to be covered and explicitly concerned themselves with subjects in which they had a special interest.

> International politics
> Political theory
> International law

International organization
Comparative government
United States foreign policy
United States government

United States diplomatic history
European diplomatic history
International history (general diplomatic history)
European history
Asian history

International economics
Comparative economic systems
Basic economics
Political geography
Economic geography
Cultural geography

Comparative social institutions
Social psychology
Cultural anthropology
Demography

Foreign languages
Comparative literature

Area study

The list cannot, of course, be considered definitive. A scattering of specialized miscellaneous courses is not included in it. Further, the items listed represent varying degrees of abstraction, and some might be included under the rubric "Others." Hence, the omission of subjects cannot be automatically regarded as meaning that the interviewees did not view them as proper subjects of study. Moreover, some items are included which are largely tools. It is nonetheless of interest to observe the admixture of relatively abstract fields and very concrete subjects. This is perhaps indicative both of the lack of a standard conceptualization of the field of international relations and the problems arising from the fact that several disciplines contribute to its study. It is interesting to note, also, that this list, derived from interviews in connection with this survey, conforms rather well with lists of fields given by writers on this subject outside the South.

It is impossible within the scope of this report to engage in a discussion of the relationship of all the various fields and courses which are or might be relevant to international relations. Hence discussion will be restricted to those relatively few subjects which elicited most comment on the part of the interviewees.

INTERNATIONAL POLITICS

International politics itself, surprisingly enough, provoked relatively little comment. The great majority of teachers of this subject would probably agree to a course content which includes (1) the nature of the international political system, (2) the factors influencing conduct within that system, (3) the objectives of states and other actors in the system, (4) the instruments by which they seek to achieve these objectives, and (5) the mechanisms and principles whereby it is attempted to harmonize the objectives. It will be seen from this description that international politics in fact embraces the whole theoretical field of international relations and may be thus an explanation for the prevailing assumption that international politics is the core of the field. It also may explain why international politics and international relations are sometimes used as interchangeable terms.

Some discussion during the interviews centered about the fact that the difficulties faced by international politics as a course apparently are the same as those which beset the field as a whole. How much emphasis is to be placed on each of the five main components? The regulating mechanisms and principles, for example, involve both international organization and international law, and both of these are complex and distinct subjects as such. The factors influencing conduct, as noted earlier, run the gamut of phenomena in the province of the humanities and social sciences. How far should the teacher go in exploring this almost limitless area? To what extent should these factors be considered in a time range; or, to put the question another way, how much historical background should be included? Should there simply be a survey of the contemporary international scene? Instruments include such complex and varied phenomena as diplomacy, neutrality (or neutralism), tariffs, war, alliances, imperialism, balance of power, unilateralism, commodity black lists, embargoes, blockades, propaganda, and subversion. To what extent should instruments, factors, and regulating mechanisms and principles be shown in operation in terms of the foreign policies of specific states?

Agreeing that choices have to be made, some interviewees suggested that the only way to solve the problem is to raise the level of abstraction. This would mean that a course in international politics could not hope to give an adequate historical background. It would use history to illustrate principles and techniques and count on the student to obtain the indispensable historical view in the history department. In the case of majors, this could be planned; in the case of others, it would have to be assumed. It would mean, too, some interviewees pointed out, that the exploration of factors would be undertaken solely in the light of their effect upon international political systems. One might expect from the teacher a reasonable familiarity with the various disciplines involved in the study of these factors. But he would present the results of his multidisciplinary studies and conclusions only as they affect international politics. He would not explore the various disciplines with his students, but he would hope that they were being stimulated to make explorations of their own. Again, it was suggested, in the case of majors this could be planned, at least to a certain extent.

According to some opinions expressed, the same considerations would hold for the regulating principles and mechanisms. International law and organization are subjects in themselves, and the majoring student ordinarily takes separate courses dealing with them. In the course in international politics, they would be treated as part of the total political scene. As far as instruments and objectives are concerned, they would constitute the essence of the international politics course, for they are *political* instruments and objectives (or politico-economic, politico-military, politico-psychological). They illustrate types and modes of political action in the international system, and, as such, they would logically be subjects for more intensive investigation in the international politics course. And they would be perhaps the least ambiguous guides to an analysis of the nature of the international system itself.

It was with some of these considerations in mind that one Southern teacher of international relations expressed the view that both the introductory course in international relations and the ultimate course in the major ought to be international politics and that they ought to be "twins." The introductory course, this teacher felt, ought to present the theoretical structure of the field, revealing the complex nature of its content and stimulating the student to undertake those special studies which would aid him in achieving a more profound comprehension of the subject. It should stimulate him to fill in the inadequacies he may have in historical background, to investigate the ambiguities of norm and reality in international law, and to study the attempts to regulate and harmonize the actions and objectives of states by means of international organization. He should seek out the factors of physical environment and human motivation that affect the decisions which are the stuff of international politics, and here the whole broad fields of the social sciences and humanities open up to him. And then, with the insights he has gained from his special studies, he should return to the problems of international politics with a more sophisticated understanding of their ramifications, testing that understanding in terms of the empirical study of specific foreign policies and conduct at the international level. In addition, this international relations teacher concluded, the student would have the opportunity to consider the philosophical and ethical issues which achieve critical importance in the study of the causes and conditions of war and peace.

POLITICAL THEORY

It is interesting that the problem of a philosophy, or theory, of international relations evoked more discussion than the subject of international politics itself. It was a common complaint that the standard courses in political theory paid far too little attention to politics beyond the level of the civil society. And, conversely, it was a common assertion that a theory of international relations would serve as a core to bring the disparate fields into focus. Actually, very few institutions in the South offer a course labeled "Theory of International Relations." It is true, of course, that many teachers attempt to bring theory into their various courses in international relations in the same manner that many political science teachers seek to bring political theory into the teaching of the several courses central to that subject. But in view of the general opinion that there is as yet no systematic theory of international relations, it may be well to consider views as to the desirability of a specific course which would devote itself to explicit analysis and formulation of theoretical propositions.

Some interviewees denied that political theorists have been lax in their attention to interstate relations. But far more expressed viewpoints such as that of a political scientist who said: "Apparently we have not developed a theory of international relations to the same extent as a theory of government in regard to its internal functions. Thus I doubt how much insight political theory courses can give to the student of international relations, except insofar as they give an understanding of basic human political relations." A teacher of political theory had this to say: "Political theory has no greater relevance to international relations than to any other subcourse in political science. It is more or less incidental that my political theory courses touch on international relations. I am forced into it to a certain extent in dealing with communism and fascism. I also pay some attention to international law." This situation was repeated in the words of other political theorists who, while not exhibiting a reluctance to deal more directly with the field of international relations, conceded that little was, in fact, being done therein.

Several political theorists were of the opinion that the relatively remote connection of political theory with international relations stems from the more general problem of its relation to the field of political science and that the proliferation of specializations to which political science has given rise has loosened the theoretical bonds that hold the subject together. One felt that the main difficulty lay in the tendency of theory to be a history of ideas and that in order to fulfill its obligations to political science and international relations it must also develop a functional approach. This indicates that the behaviorist school is by no means alone in advancing the argument. Generally, however, it is of interest to note that the behaviorist approach has not caused the degree of ferment in the South that it has in other parts of the country.

A number of teachers advanced the proposition that there are two ways in which political theory can give indispensable service to international relations. The first is to become the keystone of the subject by developing a theory of politics at the international level. The second, of almost equal practical—if not theoretical—importance, is to provide insight into the diverse value systems which affect the international scene. It seemed clear to many that the contributions of political theory have been more noticeable in the second category than in the first. Here the conflict of competing ideologies and the achievement of political personality by once exotic and passive civilizations have stimulated new interest in the role of ideas in contemporary political conduct. It was the opinion of some, however, that the study of international relations has not yet succeeded in assessing the importance of various ideas. As one political theorist put it, "Teachers of international relations too often assume that ideas are merely window dressing for power seeking and not an integral part of political conduct." The power orientation of many of the international relations textbooks seems to support this assertion. The success of this orientation may be in large part a reaction to the utopian period of international relations studies. But the issue raised engenders the opinion that the closer integration of political theory and international relations must come as a result of effort on the part of teachers of both subjects.

Insofar as a theory of international relations itself is concerned —that is, a theory of conduct in the international arena—there was considerable agreement that its logical point of departure is the phenomenon of political conduct in a system with no central authority. Frederick S. Dunn has written:

International politics is not merely domestic politics applied beyond national borders but has an essential character of its own. It is true that political power operates in many ways common to all social environments, but the conduct of political relationships is different in a community in which power is centralized in a single point at the top and one in which it is not. The security of the individual unit becomes a profoundly different problem and the possibility of the resort to force is always in the background.[1]

In such terms the special characteristics of alliances, balance of power, hegemony, and other political instruments and objectives in international politics become more meaningful, as do the relatively limited roles of international law and international organization.

While it is essential to distinguish between the intrastate and interstate environments, the views of many are represented by one teacher who said: "Politics occurs at all levels of organization from local to international. A methodology of political science ought to hold good at all these levels, too." A universal view of politics, it was maintained, would perhaps clear the path as well for more coherent advances from description to analysis and prediction. Both international relations and political science are, after all, concerned with training students to make wiser decisions, whether as professionals or as citizen-participants. Decision inevitably involves anticipation and prediction. If systematic study is unable to aid the individual to make better predictions and thus increase the measure of his control over or forewarning of events, it hardly can lay claim to being "scientific" study.

Finally, interviewees observed that it is in the realm of theory

1 Dunn, "Education and Foreign Affairs" in Joseph E. McLean (ed.), *The Public Service and University Education* (Princeton, N. J.: Princeton University Press, 1949), p. 132.

that the problem of moral norms in international conduct must be assayed. The concern of some Southern teachers regarding this problem has already been noted. At a time when atomic power has added new and terrible dimensions to the old problem of ends and means, the ethics of foreign policy demand sober and searching consideration.

One teacher remarked that the weakness of norms in international relations was owing "not only to a lack of authority but also to the lack of a community of values." And a political theorist expressed the belief that international relations would be a more meaningful field for political theory "if one could think of a world community sharing common values." His point was that the diversity of premises and value systems made it very difficult to erect a theoretical structure capable of comprehending this diversity. The task is, indeed, a formidable one, but it was clear to many that the task was well worth undertaking.

POLITICAL THEORY IN RELATION TO PHILOSOPHY COURSES

It seems apparent that the student of international relations needs to draw on courses offered in the philosophy department in order to grasp the relationship of political ends to the other ends of life. Yet, in responding to the written questionnaire portion of this survey, few schools listed philosophy courses as being "designed wholly or in part to give the student an understanding of international relations." One teacher of philosophy tended to place the blame for this isolation on philosophy itself which, in his opinion, had gone too much into logical analysis and "super-semantics," making its relationship to international relations, or indeed to any other field, somewhat tenuous. The same teacher expressed the conviction that philosophy was once again beginning to focus its attention on human ends and values and could thus look forward to making greater contributions to international relations.

Whether or not this diagnosis is a correct one, it seemed evident to many that there is a need for philosophical insight into a field which studies the phenomena of force, inequality, arbitrariness, and conflicting values of all kinds. Without philosophical insight, the uncomfortable facts of international relations are likely to leave the student cynical or to drive him to seek utopian solutions. In either case the student would be ill-equipped to deal with realities or with the distortions of reality by which communism and other totalitarian ideologies attempt to make their cases plausible.

INTERNATIONAL LAW

The whole problem of ends and values is closely related to the teaching of international law. An opinion shared by some of those interviewed was that international law has little meaning for the realities of international politics. Thus, instead of being central to the study of international relations, international law in the belief of many may be considered an optional specialty.

While it cannot be judged whether these opinions represent a majority viewpoint, the fact that there is doubt at all as to the role of international law is in sharp contrast to its status in former times. Professor Edgar S. Furniss, Jr., has written of the earlier days of international relations teaching that "International Law was . . . made the sum of international relations rather than an integral part." [2] Apparently there is now some question as to whether it represents even an "integral part." Perhaps this is the basis of the complaint of one international law teacher that the advocates of the power politics approach have done grave damage. The fact that international law is taught in some places solely in the law school also may have its effects.

It seems certain that the well-known condemnation of legalistic-moralistic views of foreign policy and international politics have contributed to the uncertainty surrounding the place of international law in both the teaching and the reality of international relations. Many also shared the opinion of another teacher of

[2] In Geoffrey L. Goodwin (ed.), *The University Teaching of International Relations* (New York: Macmillan Co., 1951), p. 96.

international law that the subject has been made difficult to teach because of the revolutionary changes through which it is going. Several teachers felt that, like political science, international law has been taught in too ethnocentric a manner and that its norms and rulings were too exclusively derived from the Anglo-American legal systems. One teacher said, "International law exists as a subject only in the sense that [the phenomenon of a] conflict of law exists. Basically there are bodies of national laws with international implications; there is no international law which can command fundamental agreement in a divided world. This is in some contrast to the nineteenth century when non-Western countries had not yet entered the family of nations. Now 'international law' is broken up [for example] into Communist, Fascist, Chinese, and American approaches to international law. At the same time, case books generally approach international law as though the Anglo-American concepts were *the* international law."

As remedies, some teachers have suggested that international law pay more attention to the decisions of both international tribunals and non–Anglo-American courts. Also, some have asserted that the studies of international relations students in the field of law should include comparative law and jurisprudence as well as (or in conjunction with) the traditional course in international law so that there would be greater appreciation of the different concepts of legality which clearly play an important role in international intercourse. In the light of these considerations, the teacher who restricted the meaning of international law to the existence of a conflict of laws fashioned his international law course to include "an idea of the nature of law, the differing philosophies of its nature, analogy with conflict of laws, Anglo-American concepts, and then a study of international law as conventional law."

It is not within the province of this report to go into the pros and cons of the case method versus the text method of teaching international law. Suffice it to say that there are staunch advocates of both approaches. Perhaps there will be agreement that the teaching method is less important than the issues, raised above, concerning substantive content. It may be noted that those who were critical of the traditional content of international law courses also tended to be critical of the case method, at least when used as the only device for the teaching of the subject.

A further substantive issue was that concerning the relation of law to politics. Again, it was those critical of the traditional international law course who raised the issue. One such critic described his course as being "not really a law course but part legal philosophy and sociolegal approach." The students are required to "hammer out positions among themselves on problems of extradition, state succession, and so on. Then they must defend their positions before the class, which thereupon decides on a policy." Such a procedure, this teacher felt, gave the students a better grasp of the relation of law to politics in the sense that political preference is the ultimate norm of law. Another teacher of international law sought to bring law and politics into a closer relationship by making the "legislative, executive, and judicial functions the main divisions [of his course] rather than a series of specific subjects such as war and peace, state succession, and so forth. This technique poses the basic question of how law is made at the international level."

Whatever the conflicting opinions as to the status of law in regard to politics, there was agreement that there is an intimate relationship between the two. Perhaps there will also be some agreement that this relationship will have to be more closely examined if some of the doubts about the place of international law in the international relations curriculum are to be overcome.

INTERNATIONAL ORGANIZATION

The problems which beset the teaching of international law find their closest parallel, naturally enough, in the teaching of international organization. Both subjects are particularly involved in the quest for norms of international conduct. But, in the view of some writers, this involvement perhaps inevitably brings with it the danger of premature assumptions of the existence of an unambiguous normative system. Professor Furniss has written that:

Study of International Organization [in the 1920's and early 1930's] was relatively new in the United States and, more than International Law, was inextricably intertwined with the debate over American participation in world affairs. . . . The study tended to be one of international administration, relying heavily on the League and the pre-League international unions. If this pitfall were avoided, another danger loomed: the idealistic insistence, earlier mentioned, of propagandizing the League cause. . . .[3]

In his study of the teaching of international relations in 1946–47, it was Grayson Kirk's opinion that the

aura of Utopianism which was once so noticeable in the course [in international organization] has now given way to a more systematic study of the political, legal and administrative problems which surround the creation and operation of an international organization designed to deal with matters formerly handled through diplomatic negotiation.[4]

But the difficulties which have been plaguing the United Nations have come fully to light only since Kirk wrote. Some of the weighty political problems have tended to bypass the United Nations in favor of diplomatic negotiation, a fact which seems to have created problems for the success of teaching international organization as well as for the international organization itself. Perhaps this gives meaning to the statement of one teacher of international organization that he intended his treatment of the subject to be "somber." In any case, another Southern teacher of international relations appears to believe that the utopian approach in international organization is not yet dead, and in the course of the survey there was limited evidence, particularly in the smaller schools, to support his argument.

Still another teacher expressed the opinion that there were no satisfactory textbooks in international organization—there were

[3] *Ibid*, p. 96.

[4] Kirk, *The Study of International Relations in American Colleges and Universities* (New York: Council on Foreign Relations, 1947), p. 38.

"none critical enough, and most were written while we were still in the rosy period before the full return to nationalism." And another asserted that "students tend to think that international organization can be successful only if it is universal and they don't see the significance of regional international organization." In connection with this latter proposition, it is noteworthy that many teachers criticized the teaching of international organization in terms of the United Nations alone or of the United Nations and the League of Nations alone, unless such a course constituted a special offering in addition to a general course on international organization. Their answer was to teach international organization as a generic problem of supranational or suprasovereign state organization. In this way the United Nations and the League of Nations take their place alongside international organizational efforts of the past and regional organizations past and present.

Still other teachers felt that they had to fight the tendency to get too heavily involved in pure description. One expressed the feelings of several of those interviewed when he said he found international organization very dry and difficult to imbue with "meat, bones, and color." A teacher of international organization at the graduate level deplored the circumstance that students coming to him who had taken the subject as undergraduates "were merely stuffed with facts." These critics offered various alternatives. One was to attempt to interpret international organization more in terms of political dynamics than of organizational structure. Another was to utilize the case system, as in public administration courses, and to concentrate on case studies of specific happenings in the United Nations.

The most outspoken of the critics of traditional instruction in international organization said that he did not include, in his own course, coverage of the United Nations or League of Nations structure except in the case of certain "key arrangements and oddities or deviations." In describing his course, he stated that he began it with a discussion of the problem, "What is a community?" and developed the idea that there is only a potential community on the world level since divisive rather than cohesive factors have primacy. He dealt then with the cold war, different types of diplomacy and the impact of international law and organization on them, conference techniques, and multilateral, nonuniversal organizations. In regard to the League of Nations, he treated such matters as the history of Articles 16 and 19 of the Covenant in action. In regard to international organization as such, he discussed such problems as the relative advantages of universal multipurpose and nonuniversal single-purpose organizations, the likelihood of a nation's acceptance of an international decision adverse to its interests, and the use of international organization as an instrument of national interest. Finally, he explored the proposition that the degree of ability of international organization to accommodate national interest determines the extent of authentic state support and involvement.

It is evident that this course description is another example, here applied to international organization, of the general agreement on the primacy of politics in the study of international relations. It has been noted, however, that many teachers have spoken of their difficulties in successfully subjecting international organization to political analysis. Moreover, many of the comments on instruction in international organization suggest that it is still seeking a way to elude the twin dangers of utopianism and too much emphasis on description of international administration. Nevertheless, many interviewees agreed that if the student of international relations is conceived of as a student of politics, it would be helpful to him to consider international organization in a generic sense as a technique of regulation in a political world. With this as a base, the student might go on, if his interests lay in that direction, to a more detailed study of various supranational organizations.

COMPARATIVE GOVERNMENT

Judging from the answers to the written questionnaires sent out during the survey, the place of comparative government in the teaching of international relations in the South is fairly well established (see Tables 18 and 19, pages 78–81). Many of the responding institutions reported comparative government courses as "wholly or in part designed to give the student an understanding of international relations." Some institutions, however, indicated that questions about the relationship of comparative government to international relations had caused them to decide against including comparative government in their responses. Moreover, it is possible that some of those schools which did originally include the subject may also have had doubts. One teacher of comparative government, from a school in the latter category, said the subject "involves certain modes and features of comparison that make it very different from international relations. [As a comparative government teacher] I am uninterested in the areas of relationships between states. I am interested in uniformities and differences in states and some elements of predictability deriving therefrom. . . . I would put comparative government in the middle-range of supporting subjects; it would throw some light on policy formulation, political processes, and power relationships."

This statement raises issues which seem appropriate for discussion here. First of all, it implies a primary concern with the domestic functions of government. A lack of interest in relationships between states may not mean that the "uniformities and differences in states" in regard to the conduct and control of foreign policy are neglected. But it does affirm that this aspect of a state's political life is only one of the many aspects to which the comparative study of government devotes itself. Grayson Kirk took note of this fact when he observed that

much of the material in the ordinary comparative government course is not directly pertinent [to international relations] because it deals with the minutiae of local government, judicial organization, political parties, administrative procedure, and the like. . . . Nonetheless, [Kirk added] an understanding of international relations demands a good working knowledge of the domestic political institutions of national states.[5]

5 *Ibid.*, p. 46.

It is in this sense that comparative government is, according to some, more relevant to international relations than the statement of the aforementioned teacher would indicate. Most teachers agree that it is imperative that the student of international relations know the actors on the international scene. And since it is unlikely that he could ever know all the actors in all their detail equally well, a comparative study which seeks out "uniformities and differences in states" would be of particular assistance to him. Also, it may be suggested, the international relations specialist could be of assistance to the comparative government specialist by providing insights into the way the relationships between states affect the "uniformities and differences" in the domestic political pattern.

This latter consideration impinges on another issue. Can a comparative study of government be meaningful without considering the total context in which the particular governments operate? The fact that foreign relations constitute an important part of this context makes the question of special interest to students of international relations. But quite apart from this interest, the question was raised by a number of teachers of comparative government during the course of the interview program. It was their contention that comparative government has concentrated too much on formal governmental institutions and that too little has, indeed, been done to place these institutions within a broader framework. In the words of one of these teachers, "We should not emphasize the institutional arrangements of France, for example, but the whys of French public opinion and what causes Frenchmen to divide or unite. We must go forward from comparative government to comparative politics." Sharing this viewpoint, another teacher said, "Comparative government should acquaint the student with the temperament and philosophy of people via their political institutions."

A final word should be said about the geographical focus of comparative government courses in the South. Results of the written questionnaires showed that principal emphasis was laid upon European and Latin American areas. Most neglected was the so-called "uncommitted area" of the world embracing Africa, the Near and Middle East, and South and Southeast Asia. It seems clear that much would need to be done to achieve a balanced geographical coverage.

UNITED STATES FOREIGN POLICY

To round out the discussion of the more important types of political science courses relevant to international relations, it should be noted here that many of the institutions responding to the questionnaires reported offering courses in United States foreign relations. A few of these courses were specifically labeled "the conduct and control" of United States foreign relations, and it seems likely that many not so labeled were in the same category. In addition, a number of institutions reported offering courses in American foreign relations with specific areas, most frequently Latin America.

These types of courses are apparently far less a problem to international relations teachers than those previously discussed. One of the basic types deals with the organizational structure for the making of foreign policy, and the other deals with specific foreign relations problems facing the United States. Most would agree that both fulfill real needs, and many of the courses combine the two types. Those few who did express opinions about the teaching of these courses were without exception advocates of a de-emphasis on structure in favor of an analysis of policy problems. A few of these critics, in turn, were emphatic in their belief that more should be done to relate American domestic politics to foreign policy decisions.

OFFERINGS IN POLITICAL SCIENCE

Against the background of interview discussions of what an international relations program should contain may be noted the statistical picture of courses related to international relations which were reported as offered, summarized in Tables 18 and 19.

TABLE 18

Number of Hours of Work in Each of 48 Course Categories Reported by Institutions in Groups I, II, III, and IV

Course	No. of Course Hours				
	Group I	Group II	Group III	Group IV	Total
1. International affairs	184	191	123	18	516
2. International organization and law	218	124	19	4	365
3. United States diplomacy	193	166	52	0	411
4. General political science	77	47	71	2	197
5. Comparative government	64	100	52	7	223
6. Latin American affairs	80	18	0	0	98
7. European affairs	110	62	12	0	184
8. Asian affairs	94	30	0	0	124
9. Near and Middle East affairs	25	3	0	0	28
10. Other government	48	14	3	2	67
Total, political science	1,093	755	332	33	2,213
11. General history	27	96	140	14	277
12. Contemporary history	136	105	125	22	388
13. European history	265	254	286	18	823
14. Near and Middle East history	15	9	5	0	29
15. Asian history	65	74	25	0	164
16. United States history	72	131	217	13	433
17. Latin American history	165	96	73	4	338
18. Other history	21	15	6	0	42
Total, history	766	780	877	71	2,494
19. General economics	74	39	61	14	188
20. International economic affairs	204	86	45	5	340
21. Comparative economics	32	15	13	0	60
22. United States economics	5	3	0	0	8
23. Latin American economics	88	5	9	0	102
24. European economics	38	9	0	3	50

25. Asian economics	14	16	0	0	30
26. Other economics					
Total, economics	464	173	128	22	787
27. General geography	120	77	115	11	323
28. Anglo-American geography	14	6	6	0	26
29. Latin American geography	76	28	17	2	123
30. European geography	57	34	6	0	97
31. Asian geography	37	20	6	0	63
32. Near and Middle East geography	9	2	0	0	11
33. Other geography	17	16	8	0	41
Total, geography	330	183	158	13	684
34. General social science	45	59	69	17	190
35. Comparative social science	0	17	6	0	23
36. General anthropology	32	17	6	8	63
37. Latin American cultures and institutions	18	0	0	0	18
38. European cultures and institutions	6	0	0	0	6
39. Asian cultures and institutions	3	0	0	0	3
40. Other sociology and anthropology	32	17	2	0	51
Total, social sciences	136	110	83	25	354
41. General humanities	0	24	8	0	32
42. Literature and civilization of Latin American countries	2	16	5	0	23
43. Literature and civilization of Europe	12	10	25	12	59
44. Other humanities (language; literature; civilizations)	0	26	19	0	45
45. Philosophy	21	15	17	3	56
46. Religion	21	24	9	2	56
47. Military	14	12	0	12	38
48. Other	11	66	95	3	175
Total, humanities and miscellaneous	81	193	178	32	484
Grand total	2,870	2,194	1,756	196	7,016

TABLE 19

PERCENTAGE DISTRIBUTION OF HOURS OF COURSE WORK, BY COURSE CATEGORY AND DISCIPLINE, REPORTED BY INSTITUTIONS IN GROUPS I, II, III, AND IV

COURSE CATEGORY	PERCENTAGE DISTRIBUTION OF HOURS OF COURSE WORK				
	Group I	Group II	Group III	Group IV	All Groups
1. International affairs	17	25	37	55	23
2. International organization and law	20	16	6	12	17
3. United States diplomacy	18	22	16	0	19
4. General political science	7	6	21	6	9
5. Comparative government	6	13	16	21	10
6. Latin American affairs	7	3	0	0	4
7. European affairs	10	8	3	0	8
8. Asian affairs	9	4	0	0	6
9. Near and Middle East affairs	2	1	0	0	1
10. Other government	4	2	1	6	3
Total, political science	100	100	100	100	100
11. General history	3	12	16	20	11
12. Contemporary history	18	14	14	31	16
13. European history	35	33	32	25	33
14. Near and Middle East history	2	1	1	0	1
15. Asian history	8	9	3	0	6
16. United States history	9	17	25	18	17
17. Latin American history	22	12	8	6	14
18. Other history	3	2	1	0	2
Total, history	100	100	100	100	100
19. General economics	16	22	48	64	24
20. International economic affairs	44	50	35	23	43
21. Comparative economics	7	9	10	0	7
22. United States economics	1	2	0	0	1
23. Latin American economics	19	3	7	0	14
24. European economics	8	5	0	13	6

25. Asian economics	2	0	0	0	
26. Other economics	3	9	0	0	4
Total, economics	**100**	**100**	**100**	**100**	**100**
27. General geography	37	42	72	85	47
28. Anglo-American geography	4	3	4	0	4
29. Latin American geography	23	15	11	15	18
30. European geography	17	19	4	0	14
31. Asian geography	11	11	4	0	9
32. Near and Middle East geography	3	1	0	0	2
33. Other geography	5	9	5	0	6
Total, geography	**100**	**100**	**100**	**100**	**100**
34. General social science	33	54	83	68	54
35. Comparative social science	0	15	7	0	6
36. General anthropology	24	15	7	32	18
37. Latin American cultures and institutions	13	0	0	0	5
38. European cultures and institutions	4	0	0	0	2
39. Asian cultures and institutions	2	0	0	0	1
40. Other sociology and anthropology	24	16	3	0	14
Total, social sciences	**100**	**100**	**100**	**100**	**100**
41. General humanities	0	12	4	0	6
42. Literature and civilization of Latin American countries	2	8	3	0	5
43. Literature and civilization of Europe	15	5	14	38	12
44. Other humanities (language; literature; civilizations)	0	14	11	0	9
45. Philosophy	26	8	10	9	12
46. Religion	26	13	5	6	12
47. Military	17	6	0	38	8
48. Other miscellaneous	14	34	53	9	36
Total, humanities and miscellaneous	**100**	**100**	**100**	**100**	**100**

The reader should recall that the interviews and questionnaires were separate phases in the study and that the categories in Tables 18 and 19 were derived for the sake of convenience and coherence in the presentation of the statistical data. Hence there is incomplete correlation between the categories in the tables and the subjects listed on pages 60–61 as essential to international relations programs. In fact, these tables could logically have been included in the preceding chapter rather than here. However, they contained information particularly pertinent to the interviews here described.

Attention is directed now only to the first sections of the tables, presenting the emphasis on the various course categories in the discipline of political science. Attention will be called to the subsequent sections in the discussions of the other disciplines, which follow. A few comparisons are worthy of note in the tabulation of political science offerings, though in each case they indicate trends rather than definitive findings. Table 19 shows that the proportion of international affairs courses increased as the size of institution decreased. Obviously, the reason for this lies in the lesser number of supporting courses in the smaller colleges as compared with the larger institutions.

The large proportion of courses under the general political science category for Group III may be contrasted with the amount of emphasis given such courses in the other three groups. Apparently, it was necessary for the smaller liberal arts colleges to rely upon a larger proportion of general courses because there were fewer specialized courses available, or perhaps the approach through general courses was a result of conscious educational policy.

The place of comparative government is interesting, for the proportion of courses in that category increased in the smaller colleges. The reason for this becomes apparent when one examines course categories six through nine, however. In Group I, where many specialized courses in the government and politics of various world areas are listed, the combined special area and general comparative government courses figure is 34 percent. When the same figures are added together for the other groups, the totals are lower for Group II, and still lower for the other two groups. Again, the picture is one of greater specialization at the larger universities.

HISTORY

In terms of compatability of terminology and outlook and interchange of students, history and political science departments probably are more closely linked than any other two departments with which international relations has a vital connection. This is understandable in view of the facts that history and political science have common foundations and that both have a catholicity of interests. Moreover, history has been the citadel of the qualitative and individualizing approach to human phenomena, and political science has probably shared this approach more than most other social sciences. In fact, and here some controversy enters, there are some historians who contend that there is no difference at all between the two—that political science is a part of history. Those who hold this view—and there were several encountered during the course of the interview program—apply it to international relations as well.

This is one of the reasons why there is a number of institutions in the South, as well as elsewhere, in which "international relations" is taught as "recent world history" or diplomatic history. But others, agreeing that international relations is an analytical and systematic study of conduct in the international system in terms of influencing factors, objectives, techniques, and institutions, believe that this is a misuse of the term; for history, this view maintains, is at once too panoramic in philosophy to permit concentrated analysis and too parochial and time-bound in the way in which its segments are taught to permit the universal approach which an analytical study requires. In short, despite dissenting voices, there was general agreement that history is a supporting subject for international relations and is not identical with it.

There have been many arguments over the issue of whether

the historian should concern himself with the most recent past. The date of the onset of the "most recent" is apparently also a matter of controversy. In any case, the issue of the contemporaneousness of history is a matter primarily for the historian. Further, many interviewees contended that it is less important for the international relations student to be versed in recent history than to gain the essential historical insights which underline the role of heritage, time, and the individuality of events. Because the international relations student must deal with abstractions such as nationalism, imperialism, and neutralism, he needs the sense of the concrete in all its variety, which history can give him. To achieve this objective, there is no period whose study could not benefit him.

It is generally agreed that the international relations student must gain from history, in addition to the knowledge above, considerable knowledge about the history of relations between states. Grayson Kirk has noted:

> The student must know enough of the domestic history of the great powers in modern times to be able to evaluate the interaction between domestic and foreign policy. Beyond that point his emphasis for the sake of economy of time, must be upon the history of international relations.[6]

This may be a formula which will satisfy those who agree with the statement of one Southern teacher that "Diplomatic history doesn't mean much if a student doesn't know about the internal affairs of a country." Admittedly, the formula is difficult to put into practice. But clearly the movement to interrelate national and regional histories is growing, and this may aid in bridging the gulf between domestic and diplomatic history. In view of the opinions expressed during the interviews, this movement is not only consistent with, but perhaps also has been encouraged by, the objectives of international relations students.

Answers to the questionnaires showed considerable consistency from group to group in the emphasis given various categories un-

[6] *Ibid.*, p. 42.

der the general heading of history (see Table 19). While it is true that the general history and the contemporary history categories received somewhat greater emphasis in the smaller and technical institutions, as might have been expected, certain other relationships maintained surprising consistency. The position of European history, for example, seemed to be unequivocal. With the exception of United States history, less attention generally was given to other areas by the smaller colleges than by Group I, but there was a striking additional exception in the area of Latin American history. Over 20 percent of all history hours in Group I were in this field, and the area did not assume nearly so much importance in the reports of the other groups.

ECONOMICS

One of the most difficult problems in an international relations curriculum apparently is to find a satisfactory way to integrate the study of economics. Again and again during the course of the interview program it was stated that the difficulty was that economics courses were primarily designed for economics majors. No one contended that this is not entirely proper from the point of view of economics departments. The problem, interviewees said, is that students of international relations, oriented primarily to political studies, apparently find it hard to digest and integrate essential economic knowledge in the form in which it is offered in most economics courses. On the one hand were the numerous economists as well as political scientists and international relations teachers who expressed the opinion that international relations students are handicapped by the terminology and concepts used in economics courses in which the majority of the students are economics majors. On the other hand were those whose position was exemplified by the comment of an economist that "The great problem is that 99 percent of international relations students are economic ignoramuses."

One economist, looking at the problem from the point of view of international relations, has said:

The object of instructing the international relations student in the economic field is not to make him an economist or even a hybrid combination of a political scientist and economist. The proper object is to make him a better political scientist, well equipped to deal with international relations problems by drawing upon the assistance of the economist.[7]

There was considerable agreement with this thesis among international relations and political science teachers and economists, with some dissenting opinion, particularly among economists. Whichever side of the argument was taken, however, there was all but unanimity that the international relations student is not getting out of economics what he should.

Several remedies were suggested, but the great majority of those interviewed agreed with the sense of the statement of one economist who remarked that the old term "political economy" has been too much neglected and that it has particular relevance to the kind of economics appropriate for the study of international relations. There was also agreement that the standard course in international economics does not often fall under this rubric: frequently it emphasizes such highly technical problems as equilibrium analysis and price theory or it concentrates on the mechanics of international trade. As a consequence, it was the opinion of a good many of those interviewed—both economists and non-economists—that the international relations student might benefit more by a course in comparative economic systems, for example. There was no disagreement that the international relations student needs to understand balance of payment problems, monetary problems, and the essentials of international trade theory. But he also needs to relate politics and economics, and many felt this is more efficaciously done in a study of economic systems than in the standard types of international economics courses.

These considerations raised a further problem. Just as an international relations student needs to know something of the in-

7 Klaus Knorr, "Economics and International Relations: A Problem in Teaching," *Political Science Quarterly*, December 1947, p. 553.

ternal political life of states as the main actors on the international stage, so he needs to be acquainted with their economic life. In the words of one teacher, if the student is to make a realistic analysis of a state's power, he will have to know how a nation uses its resources, its capital and labor. Using as an example American proposals for an international trade charter and organization, Professor Knorr earlier stated the problem this way:

The essential interdependence of all economic policies, internal and external, is registered faithfully—and it should also be registered in international relations instruction. How is American agricultural policy, or British full-employment policy, or Indian industrialization policy reflected in the foreign economic problems and policies of the countries concerned? Such questions are relevant to the training of international relations students.[8]

Other questions of interest to international relations students concerned economic policies and techniques. Some of the following questions were mentioned by those interviewed: What are the economic sources of political power? What are the characteristics and problems of such politico-economic weapons as import and export restrictions, cartels, economic penetration of foreign areas, embargoes, and black lists? What can be done to overcome the fears of those in underdeveloped areas who have hitherto been subject not only to economic exploitation but also to political domination? What kinds of technical assistance will be most productive for various areas? To what degree are specific countries immune from economic pressure, and what are the possibilities of retaliation? What are the prospects of specific means for regional economic collaboration? All these questions illustrate the vital importance of economics to the student of international relations. Interviewees agreed that the student who is not getting answers or being taught how to find the answers will have a serious deficiency in his training.

Kirk has remarked that the ideal solution would be to offer two different international economics courses, one for interna-

[8] *Ibid.*, pp. 560–61.

tional relations students and the other for economics students; but that this solution is not financially possible except in a few of the larger institutions if, in fact, it is desirable or necessary.[9] It may be suggested, Kirk also noted, that a closer relationship between politics and economics would be of mutual benefit. One of the economists interviewed observed that "One cannot understand why some countries follow certain economic policies without understanding their political problems." It was clear to many of those discussing these problems that if economists and political scientists both recognize and act on the need for the insights which each can give the other, economics and international relations, as well as other fields, will be the beneficiaries.

In general, all groups tended in the questionnaires to concentrate upon a few kinds of economics courses rather than to draw upon a large variety of types of courses, as in the disciplines of history and political science. Heavy emphasis was placed upon general economics courses, especially in Groups III and IV, and upon courses in the category of international economic affairs. This result does not imply that there were fewer courses available in the departments of economics; the implication, rather, is that relatively fewer kinds of economics courses were considered relevant in the sense that they were wholly or partly designed to give the student an understanding of international relations. The principal exception to this general picture was in the field of Latin American economics, to which, again, Group I apportioned approximately 20 percent of its reported offerings.

GEOGRAPHY

The role of geography in an international relations curriculum, like that of economics, is a confused one, though the problems are of a different kind. One problem seems to be the comparative isolation of geography from the social sciences in general. There was some evidence in the answers to the questionnaires that educational institutions may not be utilizing all their

9 Kirk, *op. cit.,* p. 41.

available resources for the teaching of geography in relation to international relations. Although the respondents frequently listed geography among the departments concerned with teaching international relations, they less frequently included specific courses in geography among those considered relevant to international relations.

Queried concerning these results during the course of the interview program, geographers had several explanations. One of the most frequent was that geography "straddled the fence" between the social and physical sciences and that this intermediate position left a good many social scientists in the dark as to geography's function and scope. One geography teacher said, "Our own dean told me that he couldn't see any difference between geography and geology." In the view of other geographers, the dean hardly could be blamed, because individual geography departments and geography teachers vary greatly in their emphasis, some strongly reflecting their antecedents in geology and others stressing the human factor in geography or the interaction of physical and cultural factors.

The split in geography is, no doubt, associated with the recency of its recognition as a significant university discipline. And the relative newness of the assumption of geography's importance, in turn, was cited frequently as a reason for its isolation from the other disciplines. The statement of one geographer that "A professor I know was amazed to discover that geography was taught at the college level, let alone the graduate level," was a theme with many variations heard during the course of the interview program. Its counterpart, also heard with variations, was that there is a widespread idea that geography is a grade school subject. The result of this view is that geography courses often have difficulty in drawing students from other departments. Apparently, this is particularly true of majors in arts and sciences; students from business administration or education schools are more likely to have geography courses prescribed or recommended. While it may be an extreme case, it is worth noting that one geography teacher remarked that he had had only one history student in his classes during his three years of teaching. Other teachers recounted only slightly less striking experiences.

While these may be primarily problems for geographers, they evidently have important implications for potential students of international relations. There is general agreement that geography is an essential part of the training of the international relations student: If he is studying the state-actors on the international scene, he must know the geographic bases from which they operate. He will need to know why location and topography make certain areas more strategic than others. He will need to understand the problems of boundary-making, in which geographic, political, economic, and military considerations all have a role to play. He will have considerable curiosity about the various geographer-theorists whose writings have propounded a greater or lesser degree of geographical determinism in world politics. And he will have a long list of questions about trade routes, strategic and critical resources, and many other subjects.

In order that they get this knowledge, some interviewees felt that students should be encouraged to avail themselves of the opportunities offered in the geography departments. In view of the different kinds of emphases in geography courses, however, they pointed out, it cannot be assumed that the existence of a geography course bearing an apparently relevant title will in fact be an asset to the study of international relations. Here seems to be an area where interdepartmental cooperation based on knowledge of the activities and needs of the departments concerned is of particular importance.

Questionnaire respondents in Groups III and IV apportioned in the neighborhood of three quarters of their reported hours in the field of geography to the general geography category (see Table 19). The percentage was less than half in Groups I and II, but still represented heavy emphasis upon general, in contrast to specific, courses (Table 19). In all groups, Latin American geography played an unusually important role, as compared with all other courses except those in general geography. And in Groups I and II, European and Asian geography were given some attention.

SOCIOLOGY, ANTHROPOLOGY, AND PSYCHOLOGY

Comparatively few courses in the fields of sociology, anthropology, and psychology were reported in answer to the questionnaires as being relevant to international relations. The emphasis upon general rather than specific courses was very marked, the principal exception being in courses falling under the Latin America heading reported by Group I. From this, it may be gathered that these courses were regarded, by those filling out the questionnaires, as relatively peripheral to the study of international relations. It is interesting to note that some writers on the teaching of international relations have considered these fields to be peripheral, whereas others, who have written on the subject more recently, have given them considerably more importance. The behaviorist school is active in applying the techniques of these disciplines to the study of political science and international relations. Apparently, however, there is relatively little behaviorist influence in international relations teaching in the South as a whole.

The impression gained from the questionnaire returns was confirmed during the course of the interview program. Insofar as sociology is concerned, the status of demography, from the point of view of international relations, was relatively unambiguous. Although it is offered at relatively few schools, its value as a tool subject was made clear as an aid to the student of international relations in assessing the power and policies of states in terms of their population characteristics.

Regarding more generalized sociology offerings, there was considerable agreement among sociologists as well as others interviewed that their relevance to international relations would be both more apparent and real if there were greater stress on non-American materials. A number of sociologists felt that more ought to be done in comparative social institutions in order to overcome a degree of ethnocentrism in American sociology. Such a development evidently would make studies in sociology of greater direct assistance to the international relations student than such studies are at present.

Anthropology and sociology share responsibility for work in race relations. With Asia, Africa, and Latin America more and more becoming subjects rather than objects of world politics, it is, in the opinion of many, increasingly important that international relations students have insight into the problems which arise in situations where there is a history of presumed racial or cultural inferiority or superiority. One aspect of these problems is too well-known to elaborate: the role which race relations plays in attitudes of other countries toward the United States. During the course of the interviews, however, there appeared to be evidence that the very proper concern with our own problem in the United States has brought about a certain amount of ethnocentrism in race relations studies and that the studies have been more valuable to international relations students at those places where they are being carried on in the wider context of culture contacts in the world at large.

If sociology has been intent on American materials, anthropology has seemed, to those interested primarily in international relations, to be concerned with primitive societies to such a degree that the subject has maintained only peripheral value to the international relations student. Anthropology apparently is only now beginning to deal more generally with the complex societies that play an important role in international politics, and here, as some anthropologists interviewed observed, it is facing problems of its own in mastering the masses of data and their relationships.

This discussion suggests that anthropology and sociology make their chief contribution to international relations in terms of techniques of research and ways of approaching problems. Here the student can benefit greatly, it was agreed, by being alerted to the importance of informal power structures and by acquiring the tools to measure them and their impact on the policies of states. Many contended that the empirical emphasis in sociological and anthropological methods can be of salutary influence in a field where abstraction sometimes leads to unwarranted conclusions.

Despite the fact that social psychology has been considered by some writers as an important subject for international relations students, very few of those interviewed expressed this opinion. Only a few institutions reported social psychology among their lists of courses "wholly or in part designed to give the student an understanding of international relations." In view of the role of propaganda in modern international politics and in view of the importance of questions such as the phenomenon of leadership, political and group loyalties, and cultural stereotypes, these results may be surprising.

Donald Young, in his introduction to Otto Klineberg's survey of research in the field of international relations, has written that

as yet, sociologists, social psychologists and anthropologists . . . have done little research on international behavior.[10]

Professor Klineberg writes in his own summation,

there is no doubt that the material reviewed is impressive evidence of the possibility of applying scientific method to the study of international relations. At the same time one is struck by the great complexity of the problems involved and the tremendous amount of work that remains to be done.[11]

These words give the impression that significant achievements in terms of the study of international relations by means of the techniques developed in psychology, anthropology, and sociology are a promise of the future. Since the time when they were written, however, the behaviorist school and others, perhaps not of the school but in its spirit, have become increasingly active in

10 Klineberg, *Tensions Affecting International Understanding*, Social Science Research Council Bulletin 62 (New York: The Council, 1950), p. vii.
11 *Ibid.*, p. 213.

political science and international relations. But their work is considered in an experimental stage by many in the South. It is less surprising, therefore, than at first glance that so little connection was reported between psychology, sociology, and anthropology on the one hand and international relations on the other.

LANGUAGES

A word should be said about foreign language training for the international relations student. Among international relations teachers, college language courses have been the subject of some criticism, expressed during the course of this survey as well as elsewhere, because the great majority of students come out of language courses with no real ability to use the language they have studied. Unless the student is a language major, he apparently has not enough time to achieve an authentic "working knowledge" of a foreign tongue under the present system of teaching. In the opinion of many, the so-called "army method". has been successful in training students fairly rapidly to develop some fluency in speaking. But, according to a good many language teachers interviewed, this method has not solved the problem of training for reading or dealing with a foreign language at the level of sophistication required for scholarly research or study. Thus, at least from the viewpoint of those concerned with training students in international relations, there remains a major problem regarding the college teaching of foreign languages.

Most of those interviewed expressed the opinion that training in a foreign language was of very great significance to the international relations student. Quite apart from the valuable research tool which knowledge of a foreign language provides such a student, there was general agreement that language gives a key for which there is no substitute to the understanding of the total context of a culture.

Some interviewees suggested that international relations teachers can help to strengthen the teaching of foreign languages by increasing student motivation (generally agreed to be low at present) to learn a foreign language and by suggesting material to language teachers which could make the learning of foreign languages a more stimulating experience. There is some evidence of a trend to strengthen foreign language training in the secondary and even in the primary schools. Such a trend doubtless would help considerably to alleviate the problems besetting the college teaching of foreign languages.

HUMANITIES

Except for a brief discussion of the importance of philosophy to political theory, little has been said about the whole field of humanities. Only a few institutions included courses in literature, art, and the like as "wholly or in part designed to give the student an understanding of international relations." This is quite understandable in view of the fact that training in international relations takes place within a liberal arts framework and atmosphere. The student is required to pursue studies in the arts and letters as part of his general education; for his education in "international relations" he would, under present circumstances, turn to the offerings of the social sciences emphasized by those questioned and interviewed in this survey. Thus, if the humanities are passed over briefly here, it is most assuredly not because those participating in the survey thought that international relations can be fruitfully studied apart from them.

In the responses to the questionnaires, such offerings as there were in this category tended to appear with greater frequency among the smaller colleges and technical schools than among the larger institutions (see Table 19). More than 50 percent of the few hours in these areas reported by Group I schools fell under the headings of philosophy and religion. Emphasis on the various categories in the other groups was scattered in a manner such that few general statements about emphasis can be made. It should be noted, however, that heavy emphasis was placed upon military courses in Group IV schools. Most of the courses appearing under the military heading in Group I and Group II schools were courses in geopolitics taught under the auspices of the military adjuncts of the reporting schools.

EMPHASIS ON VARIOUS WORLD AREAS

This summary includes courses whose titles indicated a foreign area orientation. The courses were drawn from all the disciplines involved.

Some work reported in various areas was classified under a non-area heading because of a conflict or overlapping in category heading. The most important example of this, in terms of number of hours involved, was in the classification of contemporary history courses under the contemporary history category, even when these courses were specified as contemporary Latin American or European history, for example. Some decision had to be made in this regard, and in either case a sacrifice to a systematic presentation of the data must account for the loss of some results in one or another category.

TABLE 20

PERCENTAGE OF TOTAL HOURS OF COURSE WORK DEVOTED
TO FOREIGN AREAS, BY GROUP

FOREIGN AREA	PERCENTAGE OF TOTAL HOURS OF COURSE WORK				
	Group I	Group II	Group III	Group IV	All Groups
Asia...................	7	6	2	0	5
Europe................	17	17	19	17	17
Latin America..........	15	7	6	3	10
Near and Middle East....	2	1	0*	0	1

*Less than 0.5 percent.

In accord with the results already reported and as shown in Table 20, the two foreign areas that received the greatest amount of emphasis were Europe and Latin America. Europe predominated generally, both because of the importance given courses in European history and because Latin America was not emphasized nearly so much in Groups II, III, and IV as in Group I. Courses concerned with Asia and the Near and Middle East followed the pattern of diminishment in the smaller and technical schools, where fewer specialized courses were available. It is apparent from the results that courses on the European area achieved the same importance in all groups, in the sense that they were reported relatively as often in Groups II, III, and IV as in Group I.

Textbooks and Readings

Participating institutions were asked to list the readings required in their principal course or courses in international relations. Of the thirty-two responding schools in Group I, twenty-seven answered this particular question for the undergraduate level and nine answered it for the graduate level. The fact that eight of the Group I schools returned no questionnaire for work at the graduate level partly explains the discrepancy in the number of responses from graduate and undergraduate divisions. In addition, many of the graduate divisions which filled out the questionnaire but gave no answer to the required reading question explained, by a note, that there were no *required* readings at the graduate level. In the other groups responses were received, as follows: fifty of the seventy-one responding schools in Group II; forty-seven of the seventy-six participants in Group III; and eight of the twelve in Group IV answered this question.

Taking into account all of the lists of required readings from all responding schools, there were approximately 400 different books and periodicals listed, ranging from textbooks to "popular" magazines. Most of these books were listed only by one or two schools. From the full list, Table 21 was compiled and shows the books named as required by four or more institutions or divisions. There were 47 such books. In addition, there were two news media, *The New York Times* and *Time,* mentioned six and four times respectively by the institutions in Groups II, III, and IV, but not in Group I.

A very rough assessment of the general content covered by the

TABLE 21: READINGS LISTED AS REQUIRED BY FOUR OR MORE RESPONDING INSTITUTIONS*

Author	Title	No. of Institutions					
		Group I, Graduate Level	Group I, Undergraduate Level	Group II	Group III	Group IV	Total
Bailey, Thomas A.	*A Diplomatic History of the American People*	6	8	21	13	……	48
Barber, Hollis W.	*Foreign Policies of the United States*	1	……	3	1	……	5
Barck, Oscar T., Jr., & Blake, Nelson M.	*Since 1900*	2	3	6	……	……	11
Bemis, Samuel F.	*A Diplomatic History of the United States*	……	2	7	5	……	14
	The Latin American Policy of the United States	1	2	2	……	……	5
	The United States as a World Power	……	1	……	2	1	4
Benns, Frank Lee	*Europe since 1870*	1	1	3	3	……	6
	Europe since 1914	……	……	3	3	1	6
Beukema, Herman, et al.	*Contemporary Foreign Governments*	……	1	2	1	……	4
Briggs, Herbert W.	*The Law of Nations*	2	4	5	2	……	13
Brookings Institution	*Major Problems in United States Foreign Policy*	3	3	3	……	……	9
Bruun, Geoffrey	*The World in the Twentieth Century*	……	……	2	2	……	4
Carlson, Fred A.	*Geography of Latin America*	……	2	2	1	……	5
Carter, Gwendolen M.; Hertz, John H.; & Ranney, John C.	*The Major Foreign Powers*	4	4	6	1	1	16
Chamberlain, Lawrence H., & Snyder, Richard C.	*American Foreign Policy*	……	……	4	……	……	4

Author	Title						Total
Cressey, George B.	Asia's Lands and Peoples		4	2	2		8
Eagleton, Clyde	International Government		2	4	1	1	8
Enke, Stephen, & Salera, Virgil	International Economics		5	5	1		11
Fenwick, Charles G.	International Law	4		6	7	1	18
Ferguson, Wallace K., & Bruun, Geoffrey	A Survey of European Civilization		2	4	2		8
Harcave, Sidney S.	Russia, A History	1	1	1	1		4
Hill, Norman L.	International Relations	1	1	3	2	1	8
	International Organization		1	4			5
James, Preston	Latin America		2		3		5
Kalijarvi, Thorsten	Modern World Politics		2	6	3	1	12
Langsam, Walter C.	The World since 1914				5		5
Leonard, Leonard L.	International Organization	4	5		1	1	11
Loucks, William N., & Noon, J. Weldon	Comparative Economic Systems	1	1	4			6
Lunt, William E.	History of England			2	2	1	5
McNair, Harley F., & Lach, Donald F.	Modern Far Eastern International Relations	1	1	5			7
Marx, Morstein	Foreign Governments		1	1	2		4
Morgenthau, H. J.	Politics among Nations	3	10	11	7		31
Morgenthau, H. J., & Thompson, Kenneth W.	Principles and Problems of International Politics	1	2	2	2		7
Palmer, Norman D., & Perkins, Howard C.	International Relations		1	5	2	1	9
Pearcy, George E., & Fifield, Russell H.	World Political Geography		4	3	2		9
Plischke, Elmer	Conduct of American Diplomacy		3	1			4

*A total of 47 readings was listed four or more times.

TABLE 21—Continued

AUTHOR	TITLE	No. of Institutions					
		Group I, Graduate Level	Group I, Undergraduate Level	Group II	Group III	Group IV	Total
Potter, Pitman B.	*An Introduction to the Study of International Organization*	......	......	2	2	......	4
Schapiro, J. Salwyn	*Modern and Contemporary European History*	......	......	1	3	1	5
Schuman, Frederick L.	*International Politics*	4	5	9	1	1	20
Sprout, Harold, & Sprout, Margaret	*Foundations of National Power*	2	5	2	2	1	12
Strausz-Hupe, Robert, & Possony, Stefan T.	*International Relations in the Age of Conflict between Democracy and Dictatorship*	2	5	5	4	......	16
Van Valkenburg, S.	*Elements of Political Geography*	......	1	1	2	1	5
Vandenbosch, Amry, & Hogan, Willard N.	*The United Nations: Background, Organization, Function, Activities*	4	5	2	......	......	11
Vinacke, Harold M.	*A History of the Far East in Modern Times*	......	1	4	......	1	6
Wallbank, Walter, & Taylor, Alastair M.	*Civilization, Past and Present*	......	1	2	2	......	5
Wilcox, Francis O., & Kalijarvi, Thorsten V.	*Recent American Foreign Policy*	1	2	1	......	1	4
Williams, Mary W.	*Peoples and Politics of Latin America*	......	......	2	3	1	6
Total		48	104	169	96	16	433
Number of different books listed as required		*20*	*37*	*43*	*36*	*16*	*47*
Number of schools or divisions listing books in each group		*9*	*27*	*50*	*47*	*8*	*141*

100

books in Table 21 reveals the distribution of subject matter presented in Table 22.

The books listed most frequently by all responding institutions were Bailey's *A Diplomatic History of the American People,* Morgenthau's *Politics among Nations,* Schuman's *International Politics,* Fenwick's *International Law,* in that order, and tying for fifth position, *The Major Foreign Powers,* by Carter, Hertz, and Ranney, and *International Relations in the Age of Conflict between Democracy and Dictatorship,* by Strausz-Hupe and Possony. The summary figures at the end of Table 21 indicate that Group I institutions, at both the graduate and undergraduate levels, listed four or five books each on the average, while institutions in Groups II, III, and IV listed two or three books each on the average. Groups II and III listed fewer *different* books in proportion to the total number they listed; that is, they tended to choose the same books more consistently than did institutions in the other groups.

TABLE 22

DISTRIBUTION OF SUBJECT MATTER OF READINGS LISTED AS REQUIRED
BY FOUR OR MORE RESPONDING INSTITUTIONS

Subject Matter	Number of Readings Listed
International relations, international politics, and international organization	13
United States diplomacy	9
European history	6
Comparative government	3
Contemporary world history	3
Latin American studies	3
Asian studies	3
Political geography	2
International law	2
Comparative economics	1
International economics	1
History of civilization	1
Total	47

Summary

As dealings between sovereign states involve many factors, it is necessary to go beyond the confines of the political science department in studying international relations. Teachers interviewed in this survey listed various courses in history, economics, geography, sociology and anthropology, and area study, as well as in political science, as subjects which international relations ought to comprise. There were varied opinions as to what the content and purposes of the individual courses should be, but international politics itself provoked relatively little comment.

While the interviews were directed largely to what international relations programs ought to contain, the questionnaires were intended to determine what actually was being offered. For this reason, and because the interviews and questionnaires were separate phases of the study, there is incomplete correlation between categories in the two groups of answers.

Courses listed as actually offered were grouped into forty-eight categories for convenience and coherence. For the whole group, the total number of hours in European history far exceeded that in any other subject. Next in order were international affairs, United States history, United States diplomacy, contemporary history, international organization and law, international economic affairs, Latin American history, and general geography. General courses tended to account for a larger proportion of total offerings in the smaller colleges than in larger institutions, because of the lesser number of supporting courses in the former.

History and political science showed closer relationship than any other two departments concerned with international relations, and there was even some overlapping such as teaching "international relations" as "recent world history" or diplomatic history. There appeared to be difficulty in the integration of economics into an international relations curriculum, and the role of geography in the curriculum appeared somewhat confused. International relations teachers had some criticism of the teaching of languages, complaining that unless students were majors in a foreign language they did not learn to use it effectively. Comparatively few courses in sociology, anthropology, and psychology were reported in answer to the questionnaire as being relevant to international relations, and only a few institutions included courses in literature, arts, and the like. In all groups, Europe received the largest proportion of hours devoted to foreign areas, although Latin America received almost as much attention in Group I.

In answer to a request for a list of readings required in principal courses in international relations, approximately 400 different titles were given, of which forty-seven were listed by four or more institutions.

5

Facilities—Human and Physical

Questionnaires directed to all the institutions requested detailed information about certain characteristics of the faculty members responsible for teaching courses in formal or informal international relations programs, or in courses designed wholly or in part to give students an understanding of international relations. The following data have been compiled on the faculty members considered to be qualified for inclusion by the responding institutions: age; teaching department; rank; date of appointment; highest earned degree; major field of graduate work; geographical location of institution where highest degree was obtained; and extent of travel outside the United States.

In order to round out the picture of instructional facilities, information was also requested about teaching loads and research activities in the institutions and about library resources, teaching aids, field trips, and scholarships and fellowships.

Characteristics of Faculties

A total of 1,119 faculty members was listed by 201 schools responding to the question about characteristics of the faculties. An analysis of responses, presented in Table 23, shows total and average number of faculty members and the range in each group. Tables 24-32 give a detailed analysis of the responses concerning each faculty characteristic.

AGE

Table 24 indicates that the general picture of the age of faculty members teaching courses related to international relations is one

TABLE 23

NUMBER OF FACULTY PERSONNEL TEACHING COURSES RELATED
TO INTERNATIONAL RELATIONS IN RESPONDING*
INSTITUTIONS, BY GROUP

GROUP	NO. OF INSTITU- TIONS REPORTING	NO. OF FACULTY MEMBERS		
		Total	Average	Range
Group I, graduate level.....	20	204	10.2	3–23
Group I, undergraduate level..................	30	317	10.6	2–23
Group II................	71	299	4.2	1–19
Group III...............	68	232	3.4	1–11
Group IV...............	12	67	5.6	1–30
Total................	201	1,119	5.6	1–30

*An institution was counted as responding even though it may not have filled out all sections of the question pertaining to faculty characteristics.

of youth, though this generalization must be qualified by the large proportion (about 25 percent) of teachers for whom no age was listed. A very small proportion of teachers were either under thirty or over sixty. The majority were in their thirties, forties, or fifties, with slighly fewer in the fifties than in the other age brackets. Group IV, constituting the technical schools, listed an atypically large proportion of faculty members as being between thirty and forty.

TABLE 24

CHARACTERISTICS OF THE FACULTY TEACHING COURSES RELATED TO
INTERNATIONAL RELATIONS: AGE

Age Group	Group I, Graduate Level (%)	Group I, Under- graduate Level (%)	Group II (%)	Group III (%)	Group IV (%)	All Groups (%)
No answer........	31	39	19	18	10	26
Under 30........	1	1	4	3	11	3
30–39...........	24	22	26	26	42	26
40–49...........	26	21	23	22	13	22
50–59...........	13	13	20	21	16	16
60 or over........	5	4	8	10	8	7
Total........	100	100	100	100	100	100

DEPARTMENTAL MEMBERSHIP

Consistent with the other findings of this survey, there were more faculty members listed from history departments and departments combining social studies than from any other field, including political science (see Table 25). Even in Group I, both graduate and undergraduate divisions reported the characteristics of more teachers in history than in any other area, though these universities also listed considerably more teachers from departments of political science than did the institutions in the other groups. In all groups, between 9 percent and 15 percent of those listed came from departments of economics; and between 3 percent and 8 percent came from geography departments. A scattering of other departments was represented, including sociology, education, modern languages, and philosophy. Others, mentioned less frequently, were English, the arts, psychology, law, anthropology, and social work.

TABLE 25

CHARACTERISTICS OF THE FACULTY TEACHING COURSES RELATED TO
INTERNATIONAL RELATIONS: DEPARTMENTAL MEMBERSHIP

Department	Group I, Graduate Level (%)	Group I, Undergraduate Level (%)	Group II (%)	Group III (%)	Group IV (%)	All Groups (%)
No answer.......	13	8	0	0	0	4
Political science...	20	21	14	2	2	14
History..........	29	29	26	24	12	26
Economics.......	14	15	9	6	13	11
Geography.......	8	8	4	3	3	6
Social studies, interdisciplinary	6	7	31	47	45	24
Other...........	10	12	16	18	25	15
Total........	100	100	100	100	100	100

RANK

Table 26 discloses a striking result of the data concerning the ranks of the staff teaching courses related to international affairs —the predominance of full and associate professors. Taken to-

TABLE 26

CHARACTERISTICS OF THE FACULTY TEACHING COURSES RELATED TO
INTERNATIONAL RELATIONS: ACADEMIC RANK

Rank	Group I, Graduate Level (%)	Group I, Under-graduate Level (%)	Group II (%)	Group III (%)	Group IV (%)	All Groups (%)
No answer.......	3	4	1	4	0	3
Professor........	49	44	44	37	27	43
Associate professor	26	26	26	28	24	26
Assistant professor	19	20	19	17	25	19
Instructor	2	4	7	4	21	5
Other..........	1	2	3	10	3	4
Total........	100	100	100	100	100	100

gether, these two ranks were filled by approximately 70 percent
of the teachers listed. The predominance of full professors was
even more marked than that of associate professors, with between
37 percent and 49 percent having attained full professorial rank,
except for Group IV. Only in Group IV was there a different distribution of rank. Here, the teaching staff was divided almost
equally among full professors, associate professors, assistant professors, and instructors. In Groups I, II, and III, 21–26 percent
of the teachers were described as assistant professors or instructors, predominantly assistant professors. Very few "other" ranks,
such as lecturer and so on, were included, except in Group III,
where a number of schools reported that there was no system of
professorial rank in use. Instructors listed by such schools were
classified in the "other" category.

DATE OF APPOINTMENT

The general youth of the faculty is probably accounted for in
large part by the relative recency of most of the academic appointments to the faculty teaching courses related to international affairs (see Table 27). A plurality of the teachers, over 40 percent,
was appointed during the 1940's, except in Group IV, where the
largest number was appointed since 1950. This result coincides

TABLE 27

CHARACTERISTICS OF THE FACULTY TEACHING COURSES RELATED TO
INTERNATIONAL RELATIONS: DATE OF APPOINTMENT

Date of Appointment	Group I, Graduate Level (%)	Group I, Under-graduate Level (%)	Group II (%)	Group III (%)	Group IV (%)	All Groups (%)
No answer.......	3	6	1	4	2	3
Before 1920......	2	1	2	3	0	2
1920–29.........	12	12	10	8	8	10
1930–39.........	17	13	15	15	10	15
1940–49.........	45	43	45	39	37	43
1950–present.....	21	25	27	31	43	27
Total........	100	100	100	100	100	100

with the greater youth of the faculty members reported by Group
IV schools. In the other groups, about 25 percent were appointed
since 1950, and about a quarter were appointed between 1920
and 1940. Very few appointments were dated before 1920.

HIGHEST EARNED DEGREE

Taking all schools together, 65 percent of the instructional
staff listed held the Ph.D. degree, as shown in Table 28. The separate group percentages ranged from 82 percent in Group I to
48 percent and 52 percent in Groups III and IV, respectively.

TABLE 28

CHARACTERISTICS OF THE FACULTY TEACHING COURSES RELATED TO
INTERNATIONAL RELATIONS: HIGHEST EARNED DEGREE

Degree	Group I, Graduate Level (%)	Group I, Under-graduate Level (%)	Group II (%)	Group III (%)	Group IV (%)	All Groups (%)
No answer.......	2	1	0	0	0	1
B. A.............	1	1	1	0	0	1
M. A............	7	11	31	43	40	24
Ph. D...........	82	77	58	48	52	65
Other...........	8	10	10	9	8	9
Total........	100	100	100	100	100	100

Generally, 8–10 percent held "other" degrees, such as the Ed.D. Most of the other teachers—ranging from 7 percent in Group I to 43 percent and 40 percent in Groups III and IV, respectively —held the M.A. as the highest earned degree. Only six individuals, or less than 1 percent of the total number of instructors reported, held no degree higher than the B.A.

MAJOR FIELD

The purpose of the question requesting information concerning the instructors' major field during their graduate work careers was to determine how many of the instructors were presently teaching in a field different from that of their principal training. From the data analyzed and set forth in Table 29, it seems safe to say that there were at least 11 percent teaching in a field different from the area of major emphasis in college. In the case of 11 percent, this fact was clearly indicated. In addition, there was a relatively large proportion of no answers to the question on major field (16 percent), and in these cases there was no means of determining whether the teaching field was the same or different. Further, a very loose interpretation necessarily was given the data in cases where the teaching departments were interdisciplinary. Particularly in Groups II and III, where there were many combined social studies departments, there were

TABLE 29

CHARACTERISTICS OF THE FACULTY TEACHING COURSES RELATED TO INTERNATIONAL RELATIONS: MAJOR FIELD OF GRADUATE STUDY

Major Field	Group I, Graduate Level (%)	Group I, Undergraduate Level (%)	Group II (%)	Group III (%)	Group IV (%)	All Groups (%)
No answer.......	32	28	3	6	3	16
Same as teaching area...........	57	61	84	88	78	73
Different from teaching area...	11	11	13	6	19	11
Total........	100	100	100	100	100	100

many teachers who had been trained in history or sociology or political science who might be teaching not only in their major field but in other social studies subjects as well. The discrepancy between training and teaching areas did not seem to vary much from group to group. However, the opportunities for additional cases of discrepancy, obscured in the instances of social studies departments, were far greater in Groups II and III than in Group I.

GEOGRAPHICAL LOCATION OF INSTITUTION
WHERE TRAINED

Between 5 percent and 10 percent of the instructional staff received their graduate training in foreign institutions (see Table 30). Most of these institutions were located in Europe, though a few were in China. From 31 percent to 42 percent were trained in graduate schools in the Southern part of the United States. The rest, a majority, were trained in the East, Midwest, and Far West, with graduates of Eastern universities predominating. The results were quite similar for all the groups of institutions surveyed.

TABLE 30

CHARACTERISTICS OF THE FACULTY TEACHING COURSES RELATED TO
INTERNATIONAL RELATIONS: GEOGRAPHIC LOCATION OF INSTITUTION
WHERE GRADUATE TRAINING WAS RECEIVED

Location	Group I, Graduate Level (%)	Group I, Under-graduate Level (%)	Group II (%)	Group III (%)	Group IV (%)	All Groups (%)
No answer.......	9	7	1	1	0	4
South...........	27	31	39	42	34	35
Non-South.......	54	54	55	50	61	54
Foreign..........	10	8	5	7	5	7
Total........	100	100	100	100	100	100

FOREIGN TRAVEL

Answers to the question concerning the experiences of faculty members in foreign travel or residence were analyzed in terms of

TABLE 31

CHARACTERISTICS OF THE FACULTY TEACHING COURSES RELATED TO
INTERNATIONAL RELATIONS: TIME SPENT OUTSIDE THE UNITED STATES

Length of Sojourn	Group I, Graduate Level (%)	Group I, Under-graduate Level (%)	Group II (%)	Group III (%)	Group IV (%)	All Groups (%)
No answer.......	18	17	38	40	39	29
None	35	38	32	35	37	35
0–2 years........	19	22	17	14	18	18
3 years or more...	28	23	13	11	6	18
Total........	100	100	100	100	100	100

the number of countries visited or lived in and the length of time
spent outside the United States as shown in Tables 31 and 32.
Roughly a third of the teachers seemed to have had no travel experience at all. On the other hand, 33 percent to 46 percent had
traveled or lived in three or more countries. In Groups II, III,
and IV, only 6 percent to 13 percent had been outside the country more than three years. In Group I, roughly a quarter of the
teachers had been in foreign countries for at least three years.

Interpretation of the figures is made difficult by the fact that
a large proportion of the faculty did not indicate the length of
time spent in foreign countries, and many did not answer the

TABLE 32

CHARACTERISTICS OF THE FACULTY TEACHING COURSES RELATED TO
INTERNATIONAL RELATIONS: NUMBER OF COUNTRIES VISITED

No. of Countries	Group I, Graduate Level (%)	Group I, Under-graduate Level (%)	Group II (%)	Group III (%)	Group IV (%)	All Groups (%)
No answer.......	9	19	10	12	5	13
None...........	33	37	33	35	37	34
1–2 countries.....	12	9	20	18	25	16
3 or more countries	46	35	37	35	33	37
Total........	100	100	100	100	100	100

question on travel at all. Generally, it seems fair to say that about 50 percent had been outside the country for at least some time, and that about half of these in Group I and 10–25 percent of these in the other groups had been out of the country for three or more years. Much of the shorter travel was in Canada, Mexico, and Central and South America, although there were a great many visits to Europe. Most of the faculty people who had spent many years elsewhere had lived in Europe, though there were a few who had lived or been born in the Far East.

Teaching Load

There were striking differences between groups of institutions regarding the number of hours taught per week by faculty teaching courses in or related to international relations, as shown in Table 33. Throughout all groups, there were relatively few who taught six hours or less, the proportion ranging from 5 percent in Group III to 13 percent in Group I. A larger proportion of the faculty in the Group I institutions, both graduate and undergraduate divisions, taught seven to nine hours a week (26 and 18 percent, respectively); but only 4–6 percent of the faculty in the other groups taught as little as seven to nine hours weekly.

The teaching load most characteristic of the Group I faculty

TABLE 33

TEACHING LOAD OF FACULTY MEMBERS GIVING COURSES RELATED
TO INTERNATIONAL RELATIONS

Teaching Load	Group I, Graduate Level (%)	Group I, Under-graduate Level (%)	Group II (%)	Group III (%)	Group IV (%)	All Groups (%)
No answer.......	17	22	1	6	0	11
0–6 hours........	13	12	11	5	9	10
7–9 hours........	26	18	5	4	6	13
10–12 hours......	34	31	29	17	51	29
13–15 hours......	9	16	50	65	24	34
16 or more hours..	1	1	4	3	10	3
Total........	100	100	100	100	100	100

members was ten to twelve hours. Although only one third clearly indicated this, the figure probably would have been much higher had there not been a high percentage (17 and 22 percent) of "no answers" to the teaching load question by universities in Group I. In Groups II and III, the number of hours most characteristic of the teaching load was from thirteen to fifteen hours. In the Group IV schools, the modal teaching load was between ten and twelve hours, as in the Group I schools; but there were many in the thirteen- to fifteen-hour bracket, and an atypically large percentage (10 percent) teaching sixteen hours or more.

Considering the results in another way, only 10–17 percent of the faculty in Group I institutions taught more than twelve hours a week. In Groups II, III, and IV, 54 percent, 68 percent, and 34 percent, respectively, taught thirteen or more hours per week.

Research Activities Pertaining to International Relations

The Group I and Group II institutions participating in the survey were asked to list the research work pertaining to international relations completed during the past five years (1948–53) by faculty and graduate students teaching courses wholly or partly designed to give students an understanding of international relations. Table 34 gives a summary description of the research work reported.

Nearly all the institutions in Group I, but less than one third of those in Group II, reported some research activity. Group I universities reported an average of twenty research studies each; but this figure is not representative as there were three schools which reported over fifty (one reported 109) and these raised the average far above the more typical figure, which lay below ten. The average number of works reported by Group II institutions was four, and in this case the average represents fairly well the typical response to this question from colleges in that group.

The tendency to draw heavily from the discipline of history

TABLE 34

Research Pertaining to International Relations by Faculty Members and Graduate Students in Institutions in Groups I and II, 1948–53

DESCRIPTION OF ACTIVITY	RESEARCH ACTIVITIES IN			
	Group I		Group II	
Number of institutions responding	24		22	
Number of research activities reported	479		85	
Number of different researchers reported	239		42	
	No.	Percent	No.	Percent
A. Departmental membership of researcher:				
Political science	166	35	15	18
History	172	36	16	19
Economics	57	12	3	3
Geography	40	8	0	0
Social sciences	19	4	0	0
Law	12	2	0	0
Other*	13	3	51	60
Total	479	100	85	100
B. Type of work:				
Book	80	17	24	28
Monograph	34	7	4	5
Articles†	233	49	41	48
Theses or dissertations	132	27	16	19
Total	479	100	85	100
C. Subject:				
United States	50	10	6	7
Europe	154	32	17	20
Latin America	90	19	9	11
Asia	55	12	13	15
Middle East	14	3	3	3
Other	17	4	9	11
Combined world areas and international organizations	71	15	26	31
Theory	26	5	1	1
Unclassified	2	0‡	1	1
Total	479	100	85	100
D. Number published, total	*229*	*48*	*39*	*46*

*In the Group I institutions, "other" departments were education, Latin American studies, philosophy, marketing. language. In the Group II institutions, "other" departments consisted principally of combined social studies departments.

†Includes chapters, reviews, papers, reports, etc.

‡Less than 0.5 percent.

for work in international relations is as apparent in the figures on research as in figures on courses. Perhaps it is even more noteworthy in the case of research activities than elsewhere because, in this instance, the universities in Group I reported as much work emanating from history departments as from the political science and government departments. In the other survey assessments of activities, the Group I institutions have been the sole exception to the general predominance of history, reporting more work in political science.

Most of the research reported was not prepared for publication in book form. It is interesting to note that a larger proportion of books was reported by Group II institutions than by those in Group I, although the great variation in the number of responses by Group I universities leaves the result open to several interpretations.

The assessment of subject matter is very rough. Much of the research reported apparently dealt with theory, but only those which did not indicate concern with a particular world area or areas were classified as theory. It may be worthy of note that a larger percentage of research pertaining to Asia was reported by the Group II institutions than by those in Group I, and, further, that over half of the research work on Asia reported by Group I institutions was conducted at one institution.

Of the total number of works reported, a little less than half had been published. The rest either were completed research or completed and in manuscript form.

Special Facilities

Questions directed to institutions in Groups I and II sought to determine what resources were available in addition to the basic curricula, courses, and texts for the study of international affairs and related subjects. In general, answers in the affirmative, specifying such resources, were rare. Most of the results, therefore, are presented in nontabular form, and these follow below.

LIBRARY RESOURCES

Following is the wording of the question on library resources:

With regard to the library resources in international relations:

1. Do you have a special collection or library? Yes_____ No_____
2. If yes, please give the approximate number of books available._____
3. Is it separately organized and administered? Yes_____ No_____

Approximately 85 or 90 percent (depending upon the group) of the institutions either answered these questions negatively or omitted the answers in the returned questionnaires. Even among the 10 or 15 percent answering the first question above affirmatively, there seemed to be considerable confusion about the meaning of the question.

Specifically, three of the graduate divisions among the Group I universities indicated a special collection or library. Of these, one institution stated that the library or collection was organized separately, but it failed to indicate the approximate number of books. The other two institutions indicated there was no separate organization. They listed the sizes of the collections as 425 and 110,000 books, respectively.

In addition to these three special collections or libraries, which were indicated as available at the undergraduate level also at each of the institutions, there were two additional universities in Group I that indicated such resources at the undergraduate level. One of these declared that its collection of 1,000 books was partially separately organized. The other indicated its library of 500 was not separately administered.

One or two respondents, in addition to those mentioned above, made separate notations that there were collections of United Nations documents. Separate mention also was made in one instance of an international law collection and in another instance of an area studies collection. None of these collections was considered by the responding institutions to be applicable as an answer to the question as asked.

Among the Group II colleges, nine indicated they had special collections or libraries. (A tenth indicated that there formerly was a special collection but that it had since been classified along with other books in the library.) One of the nine colleges specified that its collection consisted of United Nations documents covering the period from 1945 to 1949. Two institutions did not give the number of books involved and indicated no separate organization. A third college that indicated no separate organization did give the number of books as 300. The other five respondents in this group indicated a separately organized library or collection, with the number of books ranging from 225 to 750.

In summary of the data on library resources, it is evident that few of the Southern institutions maintain separate collections on the field of international relations. Several institutions commented marginally on the questionnaire forms that there were "adequate" resources available through the general library, and doubtless this statement applies equally to many of the institutions participating in the survey.

TEACHING AIDS

In answer to the question asking specification of "any teaching aids of particular significance for international relations," approximately 22 percent of Group I graduate schools, 38 percent of Group I undergraduate divisions, and 35 percent of Group II colleges indicated the presence of such aids. The reason for the difference between the percentage of the undergraduate and graduate divisions of Group I institutions answering in the affirmative is to be found in the fact that a greater number of graduate divisions did not answer this question. The reader will recall that several institutions in Group I did not return a graduate questionnaire at all. Actually, the same percentage, approximately 19, in both the graduate and undergraduate groups indicated specifically the absence of such teaching aids.

Table 35 presents a summary of the types of teaching aids mentioned, with indication of the group by which each aid was mentioned. Because so few teaching aids were listed, no trends revealing which aids were considered most important or which were present in the greatest quantity were observable. The frequency with which each aid was mentioned is meaningless here, therefore, and is not reported. Teaching aids are presented in alphabetical order.

TABLE 35

TYPES OF TEACHING AIDS LISTED BY RESPONDING INSTITUTIONS IN GROUPS I AND II

Type of Teaching Aid	Group I, Graduate Level	Group I, Undergraduate Level	Group II
1. Art exhibits			✓
2. Charts and graphs	✓	✓	✓
3. Field trips			✓
4. Film strips	✓	✓	✓
5. Foreign student orientation program			✓
6. Guest speakers	✓	✓	✓
7. Illustrative pamphlets and periodicals on international affairs	✓	✓	✓
8. International Relations Club			✓
9. International relations conferences			✓
10. Library		✓	✓
11. Maps	✓	✓	✓
12. Radio programs	✓	✓	✓
13. Tape and platter recordings	✓	✓	✓
14. United Nations and State Department bulletins	✓	✓	✓

A rather loose interpretation was given the term "teaching aids" by some institutions in both groups. This is evidenced by their inclusion of activities not ordinarily considered in this light, such as "guest speakers" and "International Relations Clubs." Many of the facilities considered as aids by institutions in Group II, however, undoubtedly were available in Group I institutions as well but were not considered as teaching aids. In keeping with many of the other findings reported, the Group II colleges, representing somewhat smaller institutions than those in Group I, tended to bring to bear a wider range of materials upon the general field of international relations than did the institutions in Group I, where more specialized facilities apparently were available.

FIELD TRIPS

Three respondents among the Group I undergraduate divisions, four among the Group I graduate divisions, and three among the Group II institutions indicated that field trips abroad were offered to their students. These do not include listings of visits to Washington or to the United Nations by some schools, principally those relatively close to Washington and New York.

Trips to Canada, the Caribbean area, Central America, Europe, Mexico, and South America were listed. Maximum duration of the field trips was given as three months, although most were shorter. The number of faculty members participating in the field trips ranged from one to three, and the number of students participating ranged from two to six in the Group I graduate schools; from two to ten in the Group I undergraduate divisions; and from two to thirty-nine in the Group II colleges. In no case was a field trip considered to be an academic requirement for those concentrating in international relations.

SCHOLARSHIPS, FELLOWSHIPS, AND ASSISTANTSHIPS

As an additional source of information about special facilities available to students concentrating in international relations, institutions in Groups I and II were asked to list the various types of awards available to such students, the number of each type of award available, and the average monetary value of each type of award. Table 36 summarizes the answers to this question. It should be emphasized that the awards listed were available to students concentrating on international relations but were not necessarily *exclusively* for their use.

Assuming that the respondents in Group II interpreted the question in the same light as those in Group I, there is one striking conclusion to be drawn from Table 36, namely that the Group II colleges compare very unfavorably with Group I insti-

TABLE 36

AVAILABILITY OF AWARDS IN RESPONDING INSTITUTIONS
IN GROUPS I AND II

RESPONSE TO QUESTION	NO. OF INSTITUTIONS		
	Group I, Graduate Level	Group I, Undergraduate Level	Group II
Reported awards available........	10	7	2
Reported no awards available......	5	10	33
Gave no answer.................	17	15	36
Total.....................	32	32	71
Range in number of awards available.	*2–32*	*2–208*	*1–2*
Range in monetary value of awards..	*$50–$1,250*	*$200–$1,200*	*$200–$300*

tutions in the proportion offering awards. While this pattern is consistent with the already-noted tendency for greater specialization to be available in Group I institutions, there is perhaps a wider difference indicated between the Group I institutions and those in Group II on the basis of awards available than on the basis of any other facilities compared.

Summary

The 201 institutions which responded to questions on characteristics of the faculty listed a total of 1,119 persons teaching subjects pertaining to international relations. The number per institution varied from one to thirty, the highest number, strangely enough, being reported in Group IV. By age, most of the teachers were in their thirties and forties and two thirds or more in each group held appointments dating from 1940 or thereafter. Despite the relative youth and recency of appointment, the teachers tended to hold high rank, and all groups reported more full professors than teachers in any other category. Every group reported more teachers in history than in any other single discipline, although all except Group I institutions listed the largest number in social studies interdisciplinary departments.

The proportion holding the Ph.D. degree was 65 percent for

the whole survey, ranging from 82 percent in Group I graduate schools to 48 percent in Group III. About three fourths held their highest degrees in the same fields as their major teaching areas, the lowest proportions being in Group I. Only a third of the teachers had been trained in the South, 42 percent in Group III being the highest proportion reported. Figures on foreign experience were difficult to interpret because of failure to answer some of the questions, but it would seem that about half had been outside the country, and about half of these in Group I and 10–25 percent in the other groups had been in other countries for three years or more. The modal teaching load for persons teaching courses pertaining to international relations was ten to twelve hours in Groups I and IV, and thirteen to fifteen hours in Groups II and III.

Nearly all Group I institutions, but less than a third of those in Group II, reported some research activity by faculty members and graduate students in the period 1948–53. The typical number of such activities in Group I was below ten, although three institutions reported more than fifty, and the average in responding Group II institutions was about four. Other groups were not queried on this topic.

In answer to a question whether a special collection on international relations was available in the library, 85–90 percent answered negatively or omitted a reply. The use of teaching aids was indicated by 22 percent of Group I graduate schools, 38 percent of Group I undergraduate divisions, and 35 percent of Group II colleges. However, a number of graduate schools omitted replies. Ten institutions listed field trips abroad as offered to students. The availability of scholarships, fellowships, or assistantships for international relations students was reported by only ten Group I graduate schools, seven Group I undergraduate divisions, and two Group II institutions.

6

A Test of Knowledge About International Relations

IF AN INSTITUTION assumes responsibility for giving all its students an understanding of international relations, then methods are needed for evaluating the successes and shortcomings of the processes established to attain this end. Is the way to achieve the goal most effectively a required course or courses? Are there successive courses through which the goal may be reached? Are extracurricular activities equally helpful? The answer to these questions, it is suggested, lie not in opinion but in fact: Which facilities can be demonstrated to be most effective in raising the students' level of knowledge about international relations? If it may be assumed that factual knowledge is necessary for proper consideration of foreign affairs, a measure of such knowledge—that is, an objective test of knowledge—would appear to be an important basic step.

The test method could be used advantageously to help college administrators decide which of the channels available to them might be most useful in helping to raise the nonspecializing student's level of knowledge about international relations. Over a period of time, data could be collected showing which courses were most closely associated with student superiority in the field, as measured by a test or tests. The value of such activities as field trips could be estimated by comparing two groups of students, both of which had followed the same curriculum but only one of which had participated in field trips.

A Test of Knowledge About International Relations was developed during the course of this survey with the aid of a committee at Tulane University. The intention was to utilize the test as a yardstick to measure, on a comparable basis, the level of knowledge achieved by students who had progressed through different curricula or participated in different extracurricular activities. A preliminary administration of the test and a subsequent analysis of the results by the Educational Testing Service in Princeton, New Jersey, supported the hypothesis that it, or tests similarly constructed, could prove useful in determining on a relative basis what students have learned about international relations. Although the test was designed primarily as a test of knowledge, the experience indicated that other similar measures might be devised for determining students' understanding of international relations in a broader sense, taking into account more explicitly their ability to handle abstract concepts, their attitudes, and so on.

In order that the test might be subjected to objective and rapid scoring (practical requisites of a test designed to be administered on a large scale), the questions devised were of the multiple-choice variety. The general aim of the writers of the questions was to deal with information basic to an understanding of international relations without requiring of the testees the technical or specialized knowledge acquired by international relations specialists.

The question-writers strove to achieve wide coverage in terms of geography, the past and the present, and disciplinary orientation. While the proportion of questions concerning various world areas was established in what could be only an arbitrary fashion, efforts were made to *specify* area representation rather than to allow its distribution to be haphazard. Insofar as coverage of the past and the present was concerned, the aim was to select subject matter of general significance to international affairs, without avoiding events either historical or current. The major difficulty, as one might guess, was in the selection of recent or current topics that could be evaluated with some confidence as having lasting significance. In the three years since the questions first were devised, a few of the then-current questions have become dated, but most of them appear to have retained their original significance. Finally, in regard to disciplinary representation, it would be apparent to almost anyone who read the test that questions were contributed by political scientists, historians, economists, anthropologists, linguists, sociologists, geographers, and lawyers, as well as by international relations specialists per se.

From the more than 250 questions written by the committee at Tulane, 162 were selected, with the advice and assistance of the Commission on Foreign Affairs of the Southern Regional Education Board and several other international relations specialists in institutions of higher education both in and outside the South. The test was administered, in this preliminary form, to approximately 250 students in five colleges and universities in the South.

As is the case in the develoment of any test of this type, the issue arises as to whether there is any relationship between ability to answer the questions on the test and knowledge in international relations as demonstrated by some other measure. In other words, the question is posed, "What validity do the questions have beyond the opinion—or hope—of the writers that the composite test gauges knowledge about international relations?" If a student makes a high score on the test, then, in order to evaluate the test's validity, it is necessary to demonstrate the student's relatively superior knowledge by his performance in a different situation either known or assumed also to require knowledge of international relations.

When there is no certain bench mark to use as the criterion for ascertaining validity, as is frequently the case in developing a standard test for a field of knowledge which has not been previously tested in a broad and standard fashion, it is necessary to make an a priori assumption in the selection of a validating criterion. In order to determine the validity of this particular test, *academic experience* was used as the criterion. A pretest was administered for the purpose of determining whether the questions devised could discriminate between the knowledge attained by students who had had a specific amount of exposure to courses related to international relations and those who had not. A second purpose of the pretest was to determine, for validating purposes, whether the questions could discriminate between groups of students at various class levels.

While the selection of academic experience as the criterion for validity is open to argument, there is no question about the necessity of those responsible for developing a test to deal, at some point in the developing process, with the matter of validity. To fail to do so would leave open the possibility that a high score—or a low score—on the test meant absolutely nothing.

The students to whom the pretest was administered were divided, then, into five groups: (1) a random selection of freshmen; (2) a random selection of seniors; (3) a group of "criterion" seniors comprising those who had taken certain courses closely related to or in international relations; (4) a random selection of graduate students; and (5) a group of "criterion" graduate students comprising those who had taken certain courses closely related to or in international relations.

The general results of this pretesting showed that many of the test questions discriminated quite well between criterion and random students at the same level; between random groups at different levels; and between criterion groups at different levels. That is, the seniors generally made higher scores than the freshmen; the graduate students, higher scores than the seniors. The criterion seniors scored higher than the random seniors, and the criterion graduates higher than the random graduates. All the differences were statistically significant.

The Educational Testing Service analyzed the results of the pretest and selected from the 162 questions in it the 90 best questions. In the opinion of the Educational Testing Service personnel, the test was ready for general administration and could be expected to be completed within a normal classroom period by most of those taking it.

It was not possible to go further with utilization of the test during the period when the survey was in progress, nor have the facilities and funds been available since the survey's conclusion to make possible general administration of the test. A copy of the final test is reproduced below in order that those who are interested may use it, modifying those of the 90 questions that seem to require it or utilizing the test as a suggestive model for a new one. Description of the test has been given in some detail in order that its characteristics may be known.

A TEST OF KNOWLEDGE
ABOUT INTERNATIONAL RELATIONS

Prepared by the Tulane Committee on International Affairs
in consultation with
The Educational Testing Service, Princeton, New Jersey

Do NOT make marks on the examination. Answer all questions by circling appropriate letters on answer sheet.

When you are not certain of the right answer to a question, pick the one you think is most likely to be correct.
Be sure to answer ALL questions.

---

1. The Marshall Plan
    a. had no objectives in common with the Mutual Security Agency.
    b. was administered by the United Nations.
    c. was entirely successful within the period of time set for it.
    d. had as an objective aid to underdeveloped countries.
    e. had as its major objective the economic recovery of Europe.

2. Tangier is located in which of the following geographical units?
    a. Algeria.
    b. Southern Spain.
    c. Morocco.
    d. Libya.
    e. Tunisia.

3. With respect to the League of Nations, the United States

    a. became a member in 1933 after the election of Roosevelt.
    b. was a member throughout the existence of the League.
    c. never became a member.
    d. joined but withdrew before World War II.
    e. became a member just prior to World War II.

4. The history of the Panama Canal involved a bitter dispute between

    a. the United States and Colombia because Colombia charged the United States with encouraging a revolution which detached Panama from Colombia.
    b. the United States and Japan because Japan feared the building of the Canal would result in a two-ocean American Navy.
    c. the United States and Argentina because Argentina feared the trade advantages which the Canal would give to the United States.
    d. the United States and France because the French had built the Suez Canal.
    e. the United States and Canada because of the Canadian desire for a St. Lawrence Seaway.

5. The Point Four program enunciated in January 1949 had as its stated objective

    a. the promotion of United States capital investment in Latin America.
    b. the establishment of free trade in the Western Hemisphere.
    c. the promotion of economic development of underdeveloped areas.
    d. the military protection of underdeveloped areas from Soviet expansion.
    e. the economic administration of colonial areas by the United Nations.

6. A prominent Communist who broke with Stalin and was assassinated in Mexico in 1940 was

    a. Trotsky.
    b. Lenin.
    c. Kerensky.
    d. Cárdenas.
    e. Stakhanov.

7. At the beginning of the Eisenhower administration Mohammed Mossadegh was premier of

    a. Iraq.
    b. Egypt.

    c. Iran.
    d. Jordan.
    e. Pakistan.

8. A country which has broken away from the domination of the Soviet Union is

    a. Yugoslavia.
    b. Czechoslovakia.
    c. Sweden.
    d. Austria.
    e. Finland.

9. The Boxer Rebellion occurred in

    a. Pakistan.
    b. Bulgaria.
    c. China.
    d. South Africa.
    e. Czarist Russia.

10. The Arctic portions of the globe have become increasingly important principally because

    a. large uranium deposits have been found in extreme northern latitudes.
    b. intercontinental commercial routes via the North Pole have proved economically sound.
    c. a gradual warming-up process in the earth's climate has opened new ice-free shipping lanes in the far north.
    d. large oil deposits have been found in land bordering on the Arctic Ocean.
    e. intercontinental bombing via the region of the North Pole is now practicable.

11. The Office of European Economic Cooperation (OEEC) was designed primarily to

    a. represent the work of Unesco in Europe.
    b. subsidize United States export trade.
    c. aid the unification of Western Europe.
    d. promote Western European economic recovery and political stability.
    e. reduce United States surplus in arms, grain, and other products.

12. By the peace treaties ending World War I, Palestine was

    a. established as a Jewish national state under the League Council.

b. allowed to choose by plebiscite between independence and control by Great Britain.

c. made a British mandate.

d. declared an independent Arab state.

e. combined with Syria under French protection.

13. According to the original Charter, the permanent members of the United Nations Security Council were the United States, the Union of Soviet Socialist Republics, the United Kingdom, France, and

a. Canada.

b. India.

c. Belgium.

d. China.

e. Italy.

14. Mahatma Gandhi was an Indian leader who

a. led the movement to prevent India from seeking her independence from the British crown.

b. tried to unite Hindus and Mohammedans under a single Indian religion.

c. tried by fasting and prayer to focus the attention of the world on the condition of the Indian middle class.

d. sought to achieve Indian independence with Russian aid.

e. led a resistance movement in India against British policy, looking to greater freedom for India from British rule.

15. Which one of the following statements most nearly characterizes American "isolationism"?

a. It is the opposite of imperialism.

b. It is a policy more characteristic of the Democratic party than of the Republican party.

c. It is a recurrent belief that the United States need not concern itself with problems beyond the Western Hemisphere.

d. The "containment policy" is its most recent expression.

e. It is a concept, held in common by Wilson and Roosevelt, which referred to the forced isolation of aggressor states.

16. What power do the states of the United States have to conduct foreign relations?

a. Power only over foreign commerce.

b. Power only to conduct their own affairs with foreign nations.

c. Power only over foreign maritime relations.

d. Plenary power.

e. No power.

17. The regime of Franco came into power in Spain by the

    a. election of 1935.
    b. Nazi invasion of 1941.
    c. revolution of 1921.
    d. civil war beginning in 1936.
    e. imposition of a puppet state in 1930.

18. Which of the following regions does NOT mine tin in significant quantities?

    a. Indonesia.
    b. The Malay states.
    c. The Belgian Congo.
    d. Nigeria.
    e. The United States.

19. In the twentieth-century world which of the following values is likely to command the greatest loyalty of the greatest number in time of international crisis?

    a. Religion.
    b. Class membership.
    c. Cosmopolitanism.
    d. Nationalism.
    e. Humanitarianism.

20. The form of government in Belgium is

    a. a republic.
    b. a constitutional monarchy.
    c. an oligarchy.
    d. an absolute monarchy.
    e. a federation.

21. On January 1, 1954, how many nations were there in the North Atlantic Treaty Organization?

    a. 5.
    b. 14.
    c. 21.
    d. 30.
    e. 60.

22. The best definition of an international cartel is

    a. any corporation which sells more than half its output in two or more countries.
    b. a monopolistic grouping of business enterprises operating across national boundaries.
    c. another phrase for free trade.

  d. a diplomatic alliance in the economic field.

  e. the principle of imperial preference.

23. Presidents of the United States have sometimes avoided the risk of senatorial negation of treaties with foreign countries by resorting to

  a. verbal communiqués.

  b. orders-in-council.

  c. the Articles of War.

  d. bills of attainder.

  e. Executive agreements.

24. The Charter of the United Nations was completed between April 25 and June 26, 1945, at a conference held at

  a. Dumbarton Oaks.

  b. Potsdam.

  c. San Francisco.

  d. New York.

  e. Paris.

25. Most of the United States air bases in Africa are located in

  a. Egypt.

  b. Morocco.

  c. Liberia.

  d. Nigeria.

  e. the Union of South Africa.

26. The Baltic states of Estonia, Latvia, and Lithuania are

  a. independent sovereign states.

  b. under the domination of Poland.

  c. republics of the Union of Soviet Socialist Republics.

  d. part of Communist East Germany.

  e. divided between Poland and the Union of Soviet Socialist Republics.

27. The international conference assembled after the Napoleonic wars to straighten out affairs in Europe was

  a. the Council of Elba.

  b. the Congress of Vienna.

  c. the Congress of Berlin.

  d. the Paris Conference.

  e. the Congress of Verona.

28. World War II started in

  a. 1939.

  b. 1940.

    c. 1941.

    d. 1942.

    e. 1945.

29. Among the following, the most important disadvantage which France faces in her efforts to play a leading role among continental European powers is

    a. deficiency in natural resources.

    b. lack of technical skills.

    c. disadvantageous frontiers.

    d. lack of internal unity.

    e. rapidly declining birthrate.

30. Which of the following statements about the British government is NOT true?

    a. It is a constitutional monarchy.

    b. The Prime Minister is elected in the same manner as the President of the United States.

    c. It is a democracy.

    d. Members of the House of Commons are elected by popular vote in the constituencies which they represent.

    e. The Prime Minister's tenure is dependent on maintaining a majority in the House of Commons.

31. Which of the following was NOT occupied by Japan in World War II?

    a. Indo-China.

    b. Ceylon.

    c. Malaya.

    d. Java.

    e. Burma.

32. Mau Mau terrorism originated in

    a. Kenya.

    b. Mozambique.

    c. Tanganyika.

    d. Angola.

    e. Bechuanaland.

33. Which of the following powers was NOT represented at the 1938 Munich Conference?

    a. England.

    b. France.

    c. Russia.

    d. Italy.

    e. Germany.

34. A major obligation assumed by Russia as a result of the Yalta Conference concerned

    a. adoption of a more lenient policy toward the Polish Army in exile and the Polish underground.
    b. an agreement to share military secrets.
    c. cooperation in air operations against Berlin.
    d. entry into the war against Japan.
    e. certain concessions as to the timing of the "second front."

35. The primary object of all diplomacy is

    a. to encourage international cooperation.
    b. to protect a nation's citizens overseas.
    c. to achieve peace.
    d. to promote the core interests of the state.
    e. to stop aggression.

36. Which of the following is LEAST characteristic of underdeveloped areas?

    a. Poor transportation facilities.
    b. An economy based on one or two products only.
    c. Periodic foreign exchange problems.
    d. Great dependence upon foreign markets.
    e. Diversified economy.

37. The Dardanelles are located in

    a. Greece.
    b. Bulgaria.
    c. Russia.
    d. Turkey.
    e. Egypt.

38. Which one of the following is NOT closely connected with Western European economic cooperation?

    a. The Benelux Union.
    b. The Colombo Plan
    c. NATO.
    d. The Schuman Plan
    e. The status of the Saar.

39. Which one of the following is NOT characteristic of "economic nationalism"?

    a. Restrictions on foreign investments.
    b. The establishment of tariff barriers.
    c. Increased dependence upon imports.

    d. Protection of infant industry.

    e. Import quotas.

40. The "Open Door" policy is

    a. similar to Japan's pre-1945 plans for a "Greater East-Asia Co-Prosperity Sphere" involving most of the Far East.

    b. another name for Theodore Roosevelt's "Corollary" to the Monroe Doctrine.

    c. usually associated with the liberal immigration policies in the United States prior to the 1920's.

    d. a principle enunciated by the United States at the turn of the twentieth century opposing further division of China and favoring free access to the Chinese market.

    e. the doctrine first enunciated by Franklin D. Roosevelt in reference to Japanese aggression in the Far East.

41. The number of members of the United Nations is nearest to

    a. 30.

    b. 40.

    c. 60.

    d. 80.

    e. 100.

42. "Manifest Destiny" is a slogan associated with

    a. the freeing of the Latin American countries from Spanish domination.

    b. the territorial expansion of the United States.

    c. the final collapse of Napoleon's imperial ambitions.

    d. the political necessities which forced Switzerland to follow a policy of neutrality.

    e. Mussolini's efforts to create an Italian empire.

43. That branch of the United Nations which deals with international adjudication is called

    a. the International Court of Justice.

    b. the Hague Convention.

    c. the Geneva Convention.

    d. the Security Council.

    e. the Trusteeship Council.

44. With respect to the recognition of foreign governments, the United States has followed the practice of recognizing

    a. only those governments accepted for United Nations' membership.

b. only those governments already recognized by some friendly power.

c. only those governments that have come to power by constitutional means.

d. governments that exercise actual authority in a state, with occasional refusal of immediate recognition to governments that have come to power by revolutionary force.

e. any government that exercises actual control over a state.

45. Which of the following states is NOT a member of the Arab League?

a. Syria.
b. Egypt.
c. Turkey.
d. Jordan.
e. Lebanon.

46. In the United States a low tariff has been traditionally associated with

a. the Republican party.
b. the Democratic party.
c. both the Republican party and the Democratic party.
d. neither the Republican party nor the Democratic party.
e. whichever of the two parties is out of office.

47. An American tourist in Paris who has had property stolen from his hotel should

a. report the matter to the American military attaché.
b. report the matter to the American Ambassador in Paris.
c. make no report since a non-citizen in a foreign country (an American in this case) has no legal rights.
d. institute suit against the hotel for failure to protect his property.
e. report the matter to the nearest police station.

48. A basic dispute has arisen in the United Nations General Assembly between the Soviet bloc and the Western group over a matter concerning disarmament. Which one of the following groupings of nations would be *most likely* to vote with the West?

a. Poland, Burma, India, the Union of South Africa, New Zealand.
b. France, Panama, the Philippines, Poland, Czechoslovakia, Sweden.
c. Ukraine, Guatemala, Australia, Egypt, Canada, Nationalist China.

    d. Guatemala, Bolivia, Peru, Ecuador, India, the United Kingdom, Czechoslovakia.

    e. The Union of South Africa, Greece, Norway, Luxembourg, Lebanon.

49. In the United States, export tariffs

    a. tend to restrict the sale of cheap foreign goods.

    b. account for from 2 percent to 4 percent of the income of the Federal Government.

    c. do not exist.

    d. are acceptable in the economic sense as long as they increase home production.

    e. are a part of our tariff tradition.

50. The Chinese Revolution of 1911, which established the Republic of China, was led by

    a. Lao-Tse.

    b. Chiang Kai-shek.

    c. Chou En-lai.

    d. Mao Tse-tung.

    e. Sun Yat-sen.

51. Among the following, the only organ of the United Nations to which the original Charter gives the power of enforcement is

    a. the International Court of Justice.

    b. the General Assembly.

    c. the Trusteeship Council.

    d. the Secretariat.

    e. the Security Council.

52. Which of the following is an "invisible" item of trade?

    a. The importation of silver.

    b. A high frequency radio broadcast to Russia.

    c. The good will engendered by a United States trade mission to Europe.

    d. Travel by an American in Europe.

    e. Acetylene gas.

53. The nation most dedicated to the principles of free trade in the mid-nineteenth century was

    a. France.

    b. Great Britain.

    c. Germany.

    d. Japan.

    e. The United States.

54. Which one of the following Russian governmental units borders the Black Sea?

    a. The Byelorussian Soviet Socialist Republic.
    b. The Karelian Soviet Socialist Republic.
    c. The Lithuanian Soviet Socialist Republic.
    d. The Ukrainian Soviet Socialist Republic.
    e. The Turkmen Soviet Socialist Republic.

55. Which one of the following statements about "national security" is correct?

    a. Nations following a policy of "national security" oppose aggression wherever it occurs.
    b. The concept of "national security" is an exclusively defensive concept.
    c. "National security" as an objective of policy rules out a policy of territorial aggrandizement.
    d. "National security" as an objective of policy may require a nation to expand as well as defend its territorial base.
    e. "National security" always conflicts with "collective security."

56. The "most-favored nation" clause under United States law refers to

    a. the establishment of priorities at international trade conferences.
    b. the granting of special economic privileges to the United States by another nation.
    c. the granting of special economic privileges to only one nation.
    d. the procedure whereby the National Security Council purchases strategic materials produced abroad to prevent their purchase by the Soviet Union.
    e. the promise to grant tariff concessions to a particular nation which are equal to the most favorable concessions granted to any other power.

57. During the first 12 years following World War I the United States

    a. reduced tariffs to enable its debtors to repay their obligations.
    b. first raised but then quickly lowered its tariff rates.
    c. kept the Underwood tariff in force unchanged.
    d. entered into many bilateral treaties to lower tariffs.
    e. in general, raised its tariffs.

58. Discussion of the proposed "Truman Doctrine" by the United States Congress in March 1947 was charged with special urgency because

    a. Britain would no longer aid Greece to combat Communist

rebels and both Greece and Turkey stood in danger of coming under Russian domination.

b. the Soviet Union was threatening to annex the Dardanelles and extend its influence eastward into Pakistan.

c. Britain could no longer maintain troops in Egypt.

d. Iran threatened to nationalize her oil industry.

e. the independence of Israel was threatened by the Arab League.

59. During the years immediately following World War II, the Saar Territory was controlled by

 a. Germany.

 b. the United Nations.

 c. France.

 d. Luxembourg.

 e. NATO.

60. Which one of the following does NOT have a Mediterranean coastline?

 a. Israel.

 b. Syria.

 c. Lebanon.

 d. Iraq.

 e. Algeria.

61. Under present conditions, which one of the following instruments of security implies the greatest commitment of United States power?

 a. NATO.

 b. The Monroe Doctrine.

 c. The United Nations.

 d. The European Defense Community.

 e. The Pacific Pacts.

62. During his tenure of power in the Soviet Union, Stalin's key office in the successful maintenance of his power was

 a. chief of secret police.

 b. grand marshall of the Red Army.

 c. premier of the All-Union Congress.

 d. president of the Soviet Union.

 e. secretary general of the Communist party.

63. The American reciprocal trade agreements program was instituted mainly to

 a. promote trade with the underdeveloped areas of the world.

    b. curtail trade with the iron curtain countries.

    c. provide barter between the United States and those countries which do not have sufficient currency to pay for American goods.

    d. bring about a reduction in American tariffs in return for tariff concessions granted by foreign countries.

    e. curtail trade with Communist China.

64. International commodity agreements

    a. establish stockpiles of essential materials for the alleviation of famine and industrial slumps.

    b. are not entered into by the United States since it believes in an open trading system.

    c. have few, if any, points of similarity with cartel arrangements.

    d. attempt to stabilize the world markets of raw materials that have suffered from overproduction.

    e. are necessarily bilateral in nature.

65. According to the United States Constitution, a treaty becomes effective when

    a. it has been examined by the Supreme Court and approved as not being in opposition with any constitutional provisions.

    b. the final terms are agreed upon and the treaty is signed by the representatives of the countries concerned.

    c. it has been ratified by both houses of the Congress and signed by the President.

    d. it has been ratified by three-fourths of the states of the United States.

    e. it has been approved for ratification by a two-thirds majority in the Senate of the United States and the President has ratified it.

66. As a result of the Spanish-American War of 1898, the United States

    a. annexed no territory.

    b. annexed territory from Spain only in the Western Hemisphere.

    c. annexed territory from Spain only outside the Western Hemisphere.

    d. annexed only those territories voting to join the United States in a plebiscite.

    e. annexed territory from Spain both within and without the Western Hemisphere.

67. Which one of the following statements about the "balance of power" is NOT correct?

   a. It is a concept similar in principle to that of "checks and balances" in the United States Constitution.
   b. It is a policy whereby weaker nations join to prevent another nation from gaining too great a preponderance of power.
   c. It is a policy with which Great Britain has been traditionally associated.
   d. It is an outmoded concept in international relations.
   e. It is a concept which the United States appears to be following during the cold war in its efforts to build up a strong Europe.

68. The Constitution of the United States gives the power to declare war to the

   a. President.
   b. President with the consent of the House of Representatives.
   c. President with the consent of the Senate.
   d. Congress.
   e. Congress with the approval of the President and the Secretary of State.

69. The treaty generally referred to as an attempt to "outlaw war" is

   a. the Kellogg-Briand Pact of 1928.
   b. the treaty setting up the Hague Convention for the Pacific Settlement of Disputes.
   c. the treaty setting up the League of Nations.
   d. the Geneva Convention, 1906.
   e. the Charter of the United Nations.

70. *Apartheid* is a plan for the

   a. subdivision of Poland.
   b. separation of Eastern and Western Germany.
   c. separation of Communists and non-Communists.
   d. segregation of non-whites in the Union of South Africa.
   e. separation of Hindus and Moslems.

71. At present the total world population is approximately

   a. 1,000,000,000.
   b. 1,500,000,000.
   c. 2,500,000,000.
   d. 3,000,000,000.
   e. 3,500,000,000.

72. Germany's allies in World War I were

    a. Austria-Hungary, Turkey, and Bulgaria.
    b. Austria-Hungary, Turkey, and Japan.
    c. Turkey, Italy, Rumania, and Greece.
    d. Italy, Bulgaria, Austria-Hungary, and Finland.
    e. Japan, Bulgaria, and Turkey.

73. Which one of the following does NOT have a Pacific coastline?

    a. Guatemala.
    b. Venezuela.
    c. Colombia.
    d. Peru.
    e. Ecuador.

74. Which of the following is usually considered to be the "father of international law"?

    a. Benjamin Franklin.
    b. Machiavelli.
    c. Jean Jacques Rousseau.
    d. Plato.
    e. Hugo Grotius.

75. Pakistan may best be described as

    a. an Indian province.
    b. a buffer state set up by India between herself and the Union of Soviet Socialist Republics.
    c. an independent country closely allied to India by ties of race and religion.
    d. a Moslem nation which would like to join India but is prevented from doing so by British policy exerted through the United Nations.
    e. a member of the British Commonwealth of Nations in frequent disagreement with another member, India.

76. Which of the following statements concerning the policy of "liberation" is INCORRECT?

    a. It does not seek to improve the relative power-position of the United States in relation to the Soviet Union.
    b. It hopes to liberate the peoples who have come under Soviet domination.
    c. It is usually associated with John Foster Dulles.
    d. It has been given considerable emphasis in statements about foreign policy of the Eisenhower administration.
    e. It implies an intensification of psychological warfare.

77. The Portsmouth Treaty was associated with which of the following wars?

    a. The Spanish-American War.
    b. The Opium War.
    c. The Russo-Japanese War.
    d. The Franco-Prussian War.
    e. The Boer War.

78. After World War II the Sudan became an issue between Egypt and Great Britain because

    a. the British wished to incorporate the Sudan into the Union of South Africa.
    b. the Egyptians had exercised sole control over the Sudan despite the fact that the applicable treaty called for joint control with Britain.
    c. the British contended that the Egyptians had no right to joint rule.
    d. the Egyptians wanted to control the Suez Canal.
    e. the Egyptians demanded sole control of the Sudan.

79. Which of the following acts of aggression occurred first?

    a. Mussolini's attack on Ethiopia.
    b. Russia's invasion of Finland.
    c. Japan's invasion of Manchuria.
    d. Hitler's annexation of Austria.
    e. Italy's attack upon Albania.

80. Which of the following phrases accurately characterizes the constitutional position of treaties in the United States?

    a. Legally not inferior to congressional legislation.
    b. Affect only those states which approve the treaty.
    c. Must be approved by the House of Representatives.
    d. Must be approved by two-thirds of the states.
    e. No jurisdiction over internal affairs.

81. The Soviet policy toward the German invasion of Poland in 1939 resulted in

    a. a Soviet alliance with France and England.
    b. Soviet participation in the territorial division of Poland.
    c. entry of the Soviet Union into the war.
    d. strong protests by the Soviet Union over the loss of Polish independence.
    e. none of the above.

82. Under the prevailing conditions of world economics, which one of the following occupations in the United States is most likely to favor high tariffs?

    a. Automobile manufacturers.
    b. Truck farmers.
    c. Importers.
    d. Watch manufacturers.
    e. Exporters.

83. Which of the following countries comes closest to being self-sufficient in foodstuffs?

    a. Belgium.
    b. France.
    c. Italy.
    d. England.
    e. Western Germany.

84. Which of the following statements concerning the policy of "containment" is INCORRECT?

    a. It was the subject of heated debate in the 1952 presidential campaign.
    b. It seeks to build up "positions of strength" for the United States and its allies.
    c. It is often contrasted with a policy of "liberation."
    d. It is usually associated with George F. Kennan.
    e. It does not seek to improve the relative power-position of the United States in relation to the Soviet Union.

85. Which one of the following does NOT have a common boundary with Iran?

    a. The Union of Soviet Socialist Republics.
    b. Afghanistan.
    c. Saudi Arabia.
    d. Turkey.
    e. Iraq.

86. The Kuomintang is the name of the

    a. Communist guerilla organization in the Philippines.
    b. Chinese republican party founded by Sun Yat-sen.
    c. Chinese branch of the Cominform.
    d. military clique in Japan during the period between World Wars I and II.
    e. upper house of the Indonesian parliament.

87. Which of the following statements about Albania is NOT true?

   a. It borders on Yugoslavia and Greece, but not on Bulgaria.
   b. It is under Soviet control.
   c. Its relations with Greece are hostile.
   d. Its relations with Bulgaria are hostile.
   e. Its relations with Yugoslavia are hostile.

88. Yugoslavia borders on

   a. the Aegean Sea.
   b. the Adriatic and the Aegean Seas.
   c. the Black Sea.
   d. the Adriatic and the Black Seas.
   e. the Adriatic Sea.

89. Which of the following statements about the veto in the United Nations is NOT true?

   a. The United States advocates abolition of the veto.
   b. Political action by the Security Council is often stymied by the veto.
   c. The unanimity rule for the Permanent Members of the Security Council is another way of describing the veto system.
   d. The United Nations was able to take action at the outbreak of the Korean War because the Union of Soviet Socialist Republics was not present in the Security Council to cast a veto.
   e. The veto is a bulwark of Great Power sovereignty.

90. The term "extraterritoriality" is used to describe

   a. the possessions of a country which lie beyond its continental limits.
   b. the political jurisdiction of a country as exercised beyond the three-mile limit.
   c. the need of a country to expand to accommodate a growing population.
   d. the special judicial privileges given the nationals of one country who reside in another country.
   e. the colonizing activities of the great powers in underdeveloped regions.

7

Summary and Conclusions

A PRIMARY PURPOSE of this survey was to determine and to assess tentatively the resources available in Southern colleges and universities for students of international relations whether as potential specialists or nonspecialists. In this final section of the report, opportunities for specialists and nonspecialists are discussed separately and then the interrelationship of the two is indicated.

Considerations Concerning the Specialist

Only a few institutions in the South have programs specifically designed for students who want to specialize in international relations. With some significant exceptions, these programs are in the large universities. The programs have been formalized in varying degrees, apparently because, in part, there are differences of opinion concerning the degree of formalization as well as of specialization necessary or desirable. Discussions with those interviewed during the survey and the responses to the questionnaires indicated that there is not a clearly established pattern concerning requirements for the specialist even when there is agreement that there should be a special program.

The diversity of approaches to the teaching of international relations specialists in the South offers opportunities as well as problems. Because the programs generally are not formalized in fact or tradition, there is flexibility in plans and offerings. Such flexibility suggests open-mindedness and readiness to bring matters into focus, an advantage at this time when the most effective role of international relations specialists both outside and within academic institutions is not entirely clear.

145

While there is a need for people who have had some training in international relations in those governmental agencies and private organizations conducting activities outside this country, it is not clear that there is a relatively greater demand for those whose *basic specialty* is international relations than for specialists in various disciplines related to the field. Many situations, both governmental and private, require or would benefit most from personnel trained basically in fields running the gamut from language skills to engineering technology, but who also had *some* training or experience in international relations.

Partially as a result of the undefined role of the international relations specialist outside colleges and universities, and partially because of the uncertain position of international relations as a discipline clearly differentiated from other social science disciplines, there is confusion or uncertainty about the goals of international relations teaching for the specialist. Is its purpose primarily that of training a professional, like the doctor or lawyer, who will leave the academic life to pursue the practice of international relations in the service of government or business? Or is its purpose primarily that of developing a scholar who, like the historian or the political scientist, will be most likely to become a part of an academic or scholarly community as a teacher and researcher? Obviously, whether the one aim or the other is primary, there will be some international relations specialists who enter both types of activities, just as there are teaching lawyers and historians employed in government and business. But ascertaining the principal aim of international relations teaching for the specialist in an institution would appear to be essential to the resolution of the confusion about the planning of curricula in the field.

Where, then, are the people whose special field of study is international relations needed most at the present time? The results of the survey suggest that the field of education has great need for personnel in this field and that their service to education can be of utmost significance. To explain why this seems to be so requires first a discussion of the nonspecializing student and his knowledge of international relations.

Considerations Concerning the Nonspecialist

In reviewing the results of the survey that apply to students who do not specialize in international relations, it is necessary to emphasize again that the questionnaires were filled out by, and the interviews conducted primarily with, faculty members who were considered on their respective campuses to be the central figures in international relations instruction. This fact restricts to an undetermined degree the reporting of information and leaves open the question of the actual number of disciplines and courses involved in the dissemination of some knowledge about international relations among nonspecializing students. Further, whereas those whose chief interest is international relations may have recognized the applicability of various fields to problems in international relations, the survey evidence does not indicate that the faculty in these related areas have accepted as a part of their own responsibility raising the level of all students' knowledge about international relations.

In one sense, at least, the survey results seem to indicate that there is a more explicit and broader assumption of responsibility for the nonspecializing student in the schools where there are no special programs in international relations. Where some obligation for increasing students' knowledge about international relations is assumed by the institution, the responsibility necessarily is divided among representatives of several disciplines. The results showed, for example, that history departments, courses, and teachers play a larger role, quantitatively, than political science departments and personnel in the smaller institutions.

Among the specializing institutions, on the other hand, there seems to be a feeling among the faculty members outside international relations that the field is the responsibility almost wholly of the specialist teachers or departments. Concern with the task of imparting knowledge in international relations is likely to be restricted by the desire to avoid intruding upon a field considered to be another faculty member's specialty as well as by the desire to avoid duplication of effort and repetitiveness in the classroom. In such cases, it is clear that there is little opportunity for the nonspecializing student to learn about international relations except in the classroom of the specialist-teacher.

The Need for Central Consideration

Throughout this survey, there was complete agreement that international relations is a field of such importance that institutions of higher education must accept a responsibility for trying to impart knowledge about it to all students. It seems clear, however, from various assessments obtained during this survey as well as in others, that college graduates generally do not know as much as they should about international relations.

Despite this generally accepted fact, in very few places has there been an institution-wide, organized attempt to specify the responsibility for the task to be done, either in regard to courses or personnel. Should a concern for international relations pervade every classroom? Are there courses which should be required of all students? Are there several possible combinations of courses, each of which would provide students with sufficient background in international relations, whatever their major fields might be? These are questions which have been considered frequently, but seldom—if ever—have they been resolved for any institution as a whole.

This problem suggests the need, if not in every institution, certainly in most institutions, for a person or persons who can serve as a focal point for assisting in the development of institution-wide planning for teaching nonspecializing students some basic knowledge about international relations. Such a person, it may be argued, ought to be fully conversant with the field of international relations and at the same time sophisticated about the problems and opportunities in approaching international relations through other disciplines or methods.

Here, then, seems to be a significant opportunity for the institutions where special programs in international relations have been developed. Is it not appropriate to think, in considerable part at least, in terms of training international relations experts primarily for the purpose of becoming college teachers and scholars? The results of this survey strongly suggest that a most significant purpose would be served if the special programs could be directed toward graduating international relations teachers rather than, or perhaps in addition to, international relations practitioners. As a matter of fact, the majority of graduates of special programs do, at the present time, go into college teaching. The suggestion applies, therefore, not to a shift in the present pattern for most international relations specialists but to a clarification of the aim to be emphasized during the training process whereby greater recognition may be given to the goal of developing international relations teachers and increasing their motivation toward the scholarly profession.

These teachers, with numbers added to their ranks, would be in key positions at their institutions to help resolve the major problem of assuring every college graduate sufficient knowledge about international relations. In addition, the specialists could do much to assure proper training in international relations for students who are being prepared for jobs in foreign countries or for work directly associated with foreign affairs. The International Cooperation Administration, for example, has contracts with several universities and colleges, but few of those employed by the International Cooperation Administration are selected for their training in international relations. Yet it can hardly be denied that proper training in international relations would be an asset to the employees as well as to the representation of this country.

Considerations for the Future

A highly significant aspect of this survey was the response of the institutions which participated in it. The large proportion of the questionnaires returned and the eagerness of those interviewed to give careful consideration to international relations education attest to the presence of a vital interest and an appreciation of the importance of this field.

The amount of interest varied, of course, from institution to institution, partially because of varying institutional aims. But there is little doubt that the presence on a campus of at least one or two people whose major concern was with international relations helped to promote a concerted effort to resolve some of the problems. This suggests that there may be a need to make available to all institutions, and especially to those where there are no international relations specialists on the campus, someone who can be called upon from time to time to help give consideration to the task of training students in international relations and to consult on organizational and professional problems. Such a person also might encourage the development of facts, through the utilization of objective measures in the form of standard tests, concerning the most effective curricular, cocurricular, and extracurricular means of training both specializing and nonspecializing students in international relations.

Those responsible for the conduct of this survey wish to avoid making specific recommendations for action, partly because there is not yet sufficient information available to justify specific recommendations and partly because the information gathered suggests that there is no specific course of action which could purport to fit the needs of all the colleges and universities participating in the survey. On the other hand, it is evident that the task of teaching students about international relations needs to be studied by each institution through the facilities of some central group on the campus which can give consideration to the needs of all the students at the school.

If there could be established in the South an organization whose purpose would be to provide information and expert assistance to those on the separate campuses who are considering international relations education, there is little doubt that a useful purpose would be served. It is hoped that the present survey has achieved, at least to a degree, its purposes of providing a beginning in the development of information and of furnishing an added impetus to the consideration of a central problem.

APPENDIX A

Questionnaire on Graduate Programs in International Relations

QUESTIONNAIRE I, the items of which are reproduced in a compressed form on the pages which follow, was prepared by the survey staff and submitted to all higher institutions in the South which had graduate programs leading at least to a master's degree in political science (Group I institutions). It was this form of the questionnaire which served as the basis for other questionnaires used in the survey: Questionnaire II was submitted to Group I institutions for their use in describing their undergraduate programs and to Group II institutions (those offering undergraduate majors in political science); Questionnaire III was used with Group III institutions, those offering no undergraduate major in political science; and Questionnaire IV went to Group IV institutions, technical or professional schools offering no undergraduate major in political science.

QUESTIONNAIRE I

Graduate Programs in International Relations*

The purpose of this questionnaire is to obtain from Southern colleges and universities certain basic information concerning the nature and scope of their present offerings in international relations. The questionnaire is in no way intended to limit the individual institution in making an appraisal of its program in international relations. Any additional information attached to the back of this form or submitted separately at a later date will be welcome and will help us to construct a more complete picture of the status of international relations teaching and research in the South.

NOTE: *Unless otherwise indicated,* all questions refer to the academic year 1952–53.

NOTE: *For institutions having area programs, an additional questionnaire is included which should be completed separately.*

Name of Institution: _____

1. Please list the academic departments which offer courses closely related to international relations.

2a. In which department is the major portion of international relations courses offered?

2b. May a student give formal emphasis within this department or within a group of departments to a special program in international relations?
   1) Within this department: Yes____ No____
   2) Within a group of departments: Yes____ No____

   If yes, specify major department involved:
   Specify other departments involved:

2c. Please give the title, if any, of such a special program in international relations.

*For the purposes of this questionnaire, the term "international relations" is to be regarded as interchangeable with the terms "foreign affairs," "international affairs," "foreign relations," etc.

2d. How is such a special program administered?

1) By one department (name)

2) By a committee drawn from several departments (name committee and participating departments)

3) Other administrative arrangement (describe and name)

3. Please list the degrees or certificates which may be obtained from the academic department offering the most courses related to international relations or sponsoring an international relations program. Or, if there is an interdepartmental program of international relations, please list the degrees or certificates which may be obtained from it.

Academic Department or Interdepartmental Program (specify for each degree)	Degree or Certificate	No. of 1953 (including summer school) Graduates Formally Emphasizing International Relations	Total No. of 1953 (including summer school) Graduates of Department (including those emphasizing international relations)

4a. Please give the number of students in the following categories for the academic year 1952-53 (including summer school):

1) Working for a degree or certificate in international relations in an interdepartmental program....... —————

2) Concentrating on international relations within a department .... —————

3) Minoring in international relations.............. —————

4b. Please give the total number of students in the graduate school for the year 1952-53 (including summer school) —————

4c. Please give the number of faculty members giving courses related to international relations for the year 1952-53 (including summer school)........................ —————

5. Please list the courses which are wholly or partly designed to give the student an understanding of international relations (including courses which may not have been offered in 1952-53):

1) Title of Course

2) Course Number (e.g., Govt. 311)

3) How Often Offered? (every quarter, every semester, every year, every other year, infrequently)

4) Length of Course (quarter, semester, year)

5) Academic Department

6) Is This Course Required or Elective for: (indicate *R* or *E*)

    a) Concentration in international relations:

        (1) M.A.

        (2) Ph.D.

        (3) Other degree

        (4) Certificate

    b) A major in political science

        (1) M.A.

        (2) Ph.D.

        (3) Other degree

        (4) Certificate

7) Name of Instructor

8) Total Number of Students Enrolled 1952-53 (including summer school)

6. If you have syllabi and bibliographies available from your courses or program in international relations, please attach them to this questionnaire.

    In addition, please list the *required* texts and readings in your principal course(s) in international relations:

Course(s)	Title of Text or Reading	Author	Date and Place of Publication

7. With regard to the library resources in international relations:

    1) Do you have a special collection or library? Yes____ No____

    2) If yes, please give the approximate number of books available.____

    3) Is it separately organized and administered? Yes____ No____

8. Do you have any teaching aids of particular significance for international relations? If so, please specify.

9a. In the last five years, have field trips abroad been a part of your international relations offerings? Yes____ No____

9b. If yes, please give the following information on your field work program, using a separate line for each field trip.

Year	Locale	Duration of Stay	No. of Faculty Participating	No. of Students Participating

9c. Are field trips *required* of those concentrating in international relations? Yes____ No____

10. Please list the number of scholarships, fellowships, and assistant-

ships that are available to the students concentrating on international relations:

Type of Award | No. Available | Average Monetary Value

11a. How many years have your international relations courses or program been in existence?

11b. If you have a formal program in international relations, how did it come to be established? Please check the pertinent categories below and give details where appropriate:

1) Result of a curriculum study
2) Faculty specialties
3) Student demand
4) Research opportunities of the area
5) Assigned grants
6) Other

11c. Have your offerings in international relations undergone changes since 1945?   Yes___ No___

If yes, please check pertinent categories below and give details where appropriate:

1) Change in degrees offered
2) Change in course offerings
3) Change in field work opportunities
4) Change in number and specialties of faculty
5) Change in numbers, interests, and demands of students
6) Other changes

11d. Do you have any future plans for changing or enlarging your present offerings in international relations?   Yes___ No___

If yes, please describe major changes and give the dates when they will probably go into effect:

1) Change in degrees offered
2) Changes in courses offered
3) Change in field work opportunities
4) Additions or changes in the composition of the faculty
5) Other changes

12. Faculty Background—All faculty members teaching courses in a formal program in international relations, or in an informal course sequence, or in courses which are wholly or partly designed

to give the student an understanding of international relations, are to be considered here:

1) Name
2) Age
3) Academic Department
4) Academic Rank
5) Date of Appointment to the Faculty
6) Highest Degree
   a) Degree
   b) Major
   c) University
7) Experience in Foreign Countries
   a) Lived in other countries (name countries and give duration of time spent)
   b) Traveled in other countries (name countries)
8) Teaching Load (No. of hours carried per semester)

13. Research in international relations by faculty and students—All faculty members and graduate students in a formal program in international relations, or in an informal course sequence, or in courses which are wholly or partly designed to give the student an understanding of international relations, are to be considered here. Please list in the following table [here condensed into outline form] the research work which these faculty members and graduate students have completed in relation to foreign affairs during the last *five* years. (Please note under column marked "Status" whether research completed—mark *R;* whether in manuscript—mark *M;* whether published—mark *P.*)

1) Name (repeat name for each research project the person has carried out)
2) Faculty Member or Student
3) Academic Department
4) Research: Book, Monograph, Article, Thesis, Dissertation, Other (specify)
5) Title
6) World Areas Involved
7) Status (indicate *R, M,* or *P*)
8) If Research Was Sponsored, Specify Name of Sponsoring Agency
9) Publisher
10) Date and Place of Publication

APPENDIX B

List of Universities and Colleges Returning Questionnaires

Group I

*Group I comprises those institutions offering graduate programs leading to at least a master's degree in political science.**

Alabama	University of Alabama
Arkansas	University of Arkansas
Florida	Florida State University †Stetson University ‡University of Florida University of Miami
Georgia	§Atlanta University Emory University University of Georgia
Kentucky	University of Kentucky †University of Louisville
Louisiana	Louisiana State University and Agricultural and Mechanical College Tulane University
Maryland	University of Maryland
Mississippi	University of Mississippi
North Carolina	Duke University University of North Carolina
Oklahoma	University of Oklahoma
South Carolina	University of South Carolina

* Categorization of an institution was based on information published in its 1953 catalogue.

† Returned undergraduate questionnaire only.

‡ Received too late for questionnaire data to be tabulated as part of group totals.

§ Returned graduate questionnaire only.

Tennessee | †Tennessee Agricultural and Industrial State University
University of Tennessee
Vanderbilt University

Texas | †Baylor University
North Texas State College
Rice Institute
†Sam Houston State Teachers College
†Southern Methodist University
Texas Christian University
Texas Technological College
University of Texas

†West Texas State College

Virginia | †University of Richmond
University of Virginia

Group II

Group II comprises those institutions offering undergraduate majors in political science.*

Alabama | Alabama College
Alabama Polytechnic Institute
Birmingham-Southern College
Howard College
Judson College
Spring Hill College
State Teachers College, Jacksonville

Arkansas | Arkansas State Teachers College
College of the Ozarks
Henderson State Teachers College
Hendrix College

Georgia | Agnes Scott College
Mercer University
Wesleyan College

Kentucky | Berea College
Kentucky State College
Morehead State College

* Categorization of an institution was based on information published in its 1953 catalogue.

† Returned undergraduate questionnaire only.

Nazareth College
Transylvania College
Western Kentucky State College

Louisiana

Centenary College
Dillard University
Louisiana Polytechnic Institute
Loyola University
Southern University and Agricultural and
    Mechanical College
Xavier University

Maryland

Goucher College
Morgan State College
Washington College
Western Maryland College

Mississippi

Millsaps College
Mississippi College
Mississippi Southern College
Mississippi State College
Mississippi State College for Women

North Carolina

Davidson College
East Carolina College
North Carolina College at Durham
Woman's College of the University of North
    Carolina

Oklahoma

Oklahoma Baptist University
University of Tulsa

South Carolina

The Citadel
Clemson Agricultural College
Converse College
Furman University
Newberry College
Wofford College

Tennessee

East Tennessee State College
Fisk University
LeMoyne College
Middle Tennessee State College
Southwestern at Memphis
University of Chattanooga
University of the South

Texas

Austin College
Hardin-Simmons University
Howard Payne College

McMurry College
Our Lady of the Lake College
Prairie View Agricultural and Mechanical
College
Texas Western College

Virginia
College of William and Mary
Emory and Henry College
Hollins College
Lynchburg College
Mary Baldwin College
Randolph-Macon College
Randolph-Macon Woman's College
Roanoke College
Sweet Briar College
Washington and Lee University

Group III

*Group III comprises those institutions offering no undergraduate major in political science.**

Alabama
State Teachers College, Florence
State Teachers College, Livingston

Florida
Barry College
Florida Southern College
Rollins College
University of Tampa

Georgia
Brenau College
Clark College
Georgia State College for Women
Georgia Teachers College
LaGrange College
Morris Brown College
North Georgia College
Oglethorpe University
Paine College
Savannah State College
Shorter College
Valdosta State College

* Categorization of an institution was based on information published in its 1953 catalogue.

Kentucky	Centre College of Kentucky Kentucky Wesleyan College Murray State College Ursuline College
Louisiana	Grambling College Louisiana College Southeastern Louisiana College Southwestern Louisiana Institute
Maryland	College of Notre Dame of Maryland Hood College Maryland State Teachers College, Frostburg Maryland State Teachers College, Salisbury Maryland State Teachers College, Towson Mount St. Agnes College St. Joseph College
Mississippi	Blue Mountain College Jackson State College Rust College Tougaloo Southern Christian College
North Carolina	Appalachian State Teachers College Bennett College Elon College Fayetteville State Teachers College Flora Macdonald College Guilford College Lenoir Rhyne College Queens College St. Augustine's College Salem College State Teachers College, Elizabeth City Wake Forest College
Oklahoma	Central State College Langston University Northwestern State College Oklahoma College for Women Southwestern State College
South Carolina	College of Charleston Coker College Limestone College Winthrop College
Tennessee	Austin Peay State College George Peabody College for Teachers King College

Knoxville College
Lincoln Memorial University
Scarritt College for Christian Workers
Union University

Texas

Abilene Christian College
Agricultural and Mechanical College of Texas
Incarnate Word College
Mary Hardin-Baylor College
Pan American College
St. Mary's University of San Antonio
Texas Wesleyan College

Virginia

†Hampden-Sydney College
Hampton Institute
Longwood College
Madison College
Virginia State College

Group IV

Group IV comprises those technical or professional schools which offer no undergraduate major in political science.*

Alabama

Alabama Agricultural and Mechanical College
Tuskegee Institute

Arkansas

Agricultural, Mechanical, and Normal College, Pine Bluff
Arkansas Agricultural and Mechanical College

Florida

Florida Agricultural and Mechanical University

Georgia

Georgia Institute of Technology

North Carolina

Agricultural and Technological College of North Carolina
North Carolina State College of Agriculture and Engineering

Tennessee

Tennessee Polytechnic Institute

Texas

Lamar State College of Technology

Virginia

Virginia Military Institute
Virginia Polytechnic Institute

† Received too late for questionnaire data to be tabulated as part of group totals.

* Categorization of an institution was based on information published in its 1953 catalogue.

INDEX